¡NECESARIO!

PRE-CSEC Spanish

GRADES 7-9

PRACTICE PAPER II FOR THE CARIBBEAN

A THREE-YEAR WORKBOOK

LIBRO DE ESTUDIANTES

ANDRE C. BRUFF

LMH PUBLISHING LIMITED

First Edition
10 9 8 7 6 5 4 3 2 1

Editor: Dr. Adrian Mandara
Cover design, book design and formatting: Sanya Dockery

Published by: LMH Publishing Limited
Suite 10-11
Sagicor Industrial Park
7 Norman Road
Kingston C.S.O., Jamaica
Tel.: (876) 938-0005; Fax: (876) 759-8752
Email: lmhbookpublishing@cwjamaica.com
Website: www.lmhpublishing.com

Printed in the USA

ISBN:978-976-8245-84-7

CATALOGUING-IN-PUBLICATION DATA AVAILABLE AT NATIONAL LIBRARY OF JAMAICA

Dear students, welcome to ¡*Necesario*! This is a three-year workbook that you will use for the first three years of learning and studying Spanish in high school. The purpose of this workbook is to help you to read and understand Spanish well at this level as well as to be able to write it competently. The purpose of this workbook is to help you read and understand Spanish well at this level and also to assist you in improving your writing skills. The structure of the practice papers in *¡Necesario!* mirrors that of the CSEC Spanish Paper II.

The reading comprehension passages focus on the cultures of various Caribbean countries. I hope that you will find pleasure in learning about Caribbean people and our cultures.

¡Necesario! makes reference to many popular social media sites and applications. This is intended to make the items more relatable to you.

In order to do these items well, you will need to be guided by your teachers. You will also need to use concepts taught in classes and to do a lot of extra work on your own. You can use the verbs and neuter gender adjectives listed at the end of this workbook. You may also use the cognates listed at the start of the book as you consider necessary.

I hope that you will enjoy *¡Necesario!* I believe that you will do very well. Spanish is an important world language and knowing it can open many doors to success for you in the future. Learning a foreign language can become frustrating at times, but if you feel frustrated remember that you can do whatever you think and believe you can.

¡Buena suerte!

ALGUNOS PAÍSES DEL CARIBE

Banderas	Países	Nacionalidades
	Anguila	anguilano (m) anguilana (f)
	Antigua y Barbuda	antiguano (m) antiguana (f)
	Aruba	arubense (m, f) arubana (f)
	Barbados	barbadense (m, f)
	Bonaire	bonairense (m, f)
	Cuba	cubano (m) cubana (f)
	Curasao	curazaleño (m) curazaleña (f)
	Dominica	dominiqués (m) dominiquesa (f)
	Granada	granadino (m) granadina (f)
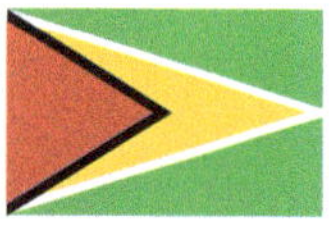	Guyana	guyanés (m) guyanesa (f)
	Haití	haitiano (m) haitiana (f)

Table of Content

BIENVENIDO vii

SÉPTIMO GRADO 1
(SEVENTH GRADE)
Funciones comunicativas 2

Term 1: Practice Test 1 3
Practice Test 2 13

Term 2: Practice Test 1 23
Practice Test 2 33

Term 3: Practice Test 1 43
Practice Test 2 53

OCTAVO GRADO 63
(EIGHTH GRADE)
Funciones comunicativas 64

Term 1: Practice Test 1 65
Practice Test 2 75

Term 2: Practice Test 1 85
Practice Test 2 95

Term 3: Practice Test 1 105
Practice Test 2 115

NOVENO GRADO (NINTH GRADE) 125

Funciones comunicativas 126

Term 1: Practice Test 1 127
Practice Test 2 137

Term 2: Practice Test 1 147
Practice Test 2 157

Term 3: Practice Test 1 167
Practice Test 2 177

LISTA DE VERBOS 187

LISTA DE ADJETIVOS CON GÉNEROS NEUTROS 194

EXPRESIONES IDIOMÁTICAS ÚTILES 195

¡No tengas miedo! – Don't be afraid!

I bet you didn't think you knew so many words in Spanish already. Try the activity below by writing the English word beside the Spanish and you will see that you already know more than 50 words in Spanish- Wow!

Palabras afines en español (Spanish-English cognates)
Sustantivos (Nouns)

Hoy (Today)		Mañana (Tomorrow)	
ESPAÑOL	INGLÉS	ESPAÑOL	INGLÉS
1. El actor		1. El accidente	
2. El animal		2. La actividad	
3. El bar		3. El área	
4. La banana		4. La cámara	
5. La capital		5. El centro	
6. El cereal		6. La cerámica	
7. El chocolate		7. El cigarro	
8. El club		8. La clase	
9. El drama		9. El continente	
10. El error		10. El diccionario	
11. El festival		11. La diferencia	
12. El final		12. El elefante	
13. El hospital		13. La familia	
14. El hotel		14. La fruta	
15. La idea		15. La galería	
16. El machete		16. El grupo	
17. El mango		17. La historia	
18. La pasta		18. La lección	
19. El perfume		19. La música	
20. El piano		20. El minuto	
21. El plan		21. El producto	
22. La plaza		22. La profesión	
23. La radio		23. La región	
24. El taxi		24. El restaurante	
25. El total		25. La televisión	

ALGUNOS PAÍSES DEL CARIBE

Banderas	Países	Nacionalidades
	Islas Caimán	caimanés (m) caimanesa (f)
	Islas Turcas y Caicos	turcocaiqueño (m) turcocaiqueña (f)
	Islas Vírgenes Británicas	virgenense británico (m) virgenense británica (f)
	Jamaica	jamaicano / jamaiquino (m) jamaicana / jamaiquina (f)
	Las Bahamas	bahameño / bahamés (m) bahameña / bahamesa (f)
	Montserrat	montserratense (m, f)
	República Dominicana	dominicano (m) dominicana (f)
	San Cristóbal y Nieves	sancristobaleño (m) sancristobaleña (f)
	San Martín	sanmartinense (m, f)
	Santa Lucía	santalucense (m, f)
	San Vicente y las Granadas	sanvicentino (m) sanvicentina (f)
	Trinidad y Tobago	trinitense (m, f)

(Seventh Grade)

Term 1 (Septiembre – Diciembre)

1. Greetings/ Farewells
2. Family
3. Likes and Dislikes
4. Self-information (name, age, etc.)
5. Describing others
6. Numbers
7. Nationality
8. Colours
9. Days/Date/Date of Birth/Birthday
10. Professions

Term 2 (Enero – Marzo/Abril)

1. Fruits
2. School (name, colours, subjects)
3. Address/ Live
4. Time
5. Animals
6. Stationery items
7. Classroom items
8. Weather

Term 3 (Abril/Mayo – Junio)

1. Seasons
2. Locating people and objects
3. House (furniture, rooms, appliances)
4. Describing things
5. Clothes

GRADE 7/ FIRST FORM

Funciones Comunicativas **Communicative Functions**

Term 1	Term 2	Term 3
1. Bidding goodbye – Chao/ Adiós/ Hasta la vista	1. Apologizing – Siento/ Lo siento	1. Advertising an event - El mejor evento/ El evento del año
2. Expressing likes and dislikes – Me gusta(n)/ No me gusta(n)	2. Identifying colours – Es verde/ gris/ azul/ amarillo/a etc.	2. Asking location of someone or something - ¿Dónde está/n?
3. Greeting – Hola / Buenos días/ Buenas tardes/ Buenas noches/ ¡Epa!/ ¡Oye!	3. Asking time - ¿Qué hora es?/ ¿A qué hora?	3. Describing something – Es interesante/ Es emocionante/ Es genial
4. Making a polite request – Por favor	4. Commending – Muy bien/ Bien hecho	4. Describing clothes – Una camisa azul/ Unos pantalones negros/ Un vestido corto.
5. Responding to thanks – De nada/ No hay de que.	5. Congratulating – Felicidades/ Felicitaciones	5. Identifying – Hay/ Tengo/ Tiene/ Es.
6. Sending special greetings – Feliz cumpleaños/ aniversario/ Navidad/ Año Nuevo	6. Expressing want and need – Yo quiero/ Yo necesito	6. Outlining seasons – Durante el verano/ el invierno/ el otoño/ la primavera / la estación lluviosa/ la estación seca.
7. Stating favourites – Mi...favorito/a es ...	7. Stating weather conditions – Hace sol/ Hace calor/ Está lloviendo etc.	7. Stating rooms and items in a house – Hay una cama en el dormitorio/ Hay un televisor en la sala.
8. Thanking – Gracias/ Muchas gracias/ Mil gracias.	8. Welcoming – Bienvenido/a/os/as	

CORRIDA DE TOROS (BULLFIGHTING)

No cometas los mismos errores

(Don't make the same mistakes)

Below are common mistakes made by students of Spanish. Please note the mistakes and the corrections given. By avoiding these mistakes, you will be sure to improve your writing skills in Spanish.

LA GRAMÁTICA (GRAMMAR)		
Inglés	**Español con error**	**Español correcto**
1. I am thirteen years old.	Soy trece años.	Tengo trece años.
2. She is a doctor.	Ella es una médica.	Ella es médica.
3. She is very nice.	Ella es muy simpático.	Ella es muy simpática.
4. I like the students.	Me gusta los estudiantes.	Me gustan los estudiantes.
5. They are father and son.	Son padre y hijo.	Son padre e hijo.

LA ORTOGRAFÍA (SPELLING)		
Inglés	**Español con error**	**Español correcto**
1. He is a teacher.	Él es professor.	Él es profesor.
2. The girl is intelligent.	La chica es intelligente.	La chica es inteligente.
3. The class is boring.	La classe es aburrida.	La clase es aburrida.
4. There are twenty students.	Hay viente estudiantes.	Hay veinte estudiantes.
5. My name is Carlita.	Mi llamo Carlita.	Me llamo Carlita.

EL ORDEN DE LAS PALABRAS (WORD ORDER)		
Inglés	**Español con error**	**Español correcto**
1. My favourite colour is red.	Mi favorito color es rojo.	Mi color favorito es rojo.
2. Welcome to my Spanish class.	Bienvenido a mi español clase.	Bienvenido a mi clase de español.
3. She is not ugly.	Ella es no fea.	Ella no es fea.
4. He is a tall man.	Él es un alto hombre.	Él es un hombre alto.

Respuestas Abiertas (Free Response)

Nombre:____________________________ Apellido: ________________________

Clase:______________________________ Profesor/a: ______________________

Fecha: ____

Duración: 90 minutos

INSTRUCCIONES

1. **Esta prueba tiene CUATRO (4) secciones. Responde a cada pregunta en este papel.**

   This test has FOUR (4) sections. Answer all questions on this paper.

2. **Sección I: Tiene DIEZ (10) situaciones. Responde a cada situación en ESPAÑOL.**

   Section I: Has TEN (10) situations. Respond to each in SPANISH.

3. **Sección II: Tiene una carta informal. Escribe la carta en ESPAÑOL.**

   Section II: Has an informal letter. Write the letter in SPANISH.

4. **Sección III: Tiene un diálogo. Rellena los espacios en ESPAÑOL.**

   Section III: Has a dialogue. Complete the dialogue in SPANISH.

5. **Sección IV: Tiene una comprensión de lectura. Responde a las DIEZ (10) preguntas en INGLÉS.**

   Section IV: Has a reading comprehension. Answer the TEN (10) questions in ENGLISH.

SECCIÓN I

LAS SITUACIONES ESCRITAS (WRITTEN SITUATIONS)
RESPONDE A CADA SITUACIÓN (RESPOND TO EACH SITUATION)

1. **Write in SPANISH the information required by each of the situations given below. Do NOT write more than ONE sentence for each situation. For some situations, a complete sentence may not be necessary. Write each answer in the space provided.**

   (a) It is 6:30 a.m. and you decide to send your Colombian friend a text message. What do you write in the message?

   (3 puntos)

   ___

   (b) While you are relaxing, you receive a text message from your Spanish-speaking friend asking you how you are doing. What do you reply?

   (3 puntos)

   ___

   (c) You are filling out a visa application form for the Mexican embassy and one of the questions asks how many persons are in your family. What do you write?

   (3 puntos)

   ___

   (d) Your new Spanish teacher wants to get to know the students better and asks each student to write one thing that he/she likes. What do you write?

   (3 puntos)

   ___

   (e) You meet a Costa Rican friend on *Instagram* and he/she wants to know something about you. What message do you send him/her?

   (3 puntos)

   ___

(f) A new student joins your school but speaks only Spanish. You want to know his/her name. What do you ask him/her in the note you send in class?

(3 puntos)

____

(g) You are doing an activity in Spanish class and one question asks students to write their favourite colour. What sentence do you write?

(3 puntos)

____

(h) It is *Family Day* at school and the Spanish teacher asks all students to write a short description of any member of their family. What do you write?

(3 puntos)

____

(i) Your friend from Argentina wants to know how many students are in your class. What do you reply in the email you send him/her?

(3 puntos)

____

(j) It is your Cuban friend's birthday. Write the text message you send him/her.

(3 puntos)

____

Sección I Total = 30 Puntos

ESPAÑA

BAILARINA DE FLAMENCO

PAELLA

CORRIDA DE TOROS (BULLFIGHTING)

SECCIÓN II

LA CARTA INFORMAL (INFORMAL LETTER)
ESCRIBE UNA CARTA EN ESPAÑOL (WRITE A LETTER IN SPANISH)

2. Using the following outline as a guide, write a letter in SPANISH of no more than 40 – 50 words.

YOU WILL BE PENALIZED FOR DISREGARDING THESE INSTRUCTIONS.

Write a letter to your new friend who lives in Ecuador telling him/her about yourself. Include:

(i) your name, age, birthday and nationality

(ii) two (2) or more descriptions of yourself

(iii) your favourite actor

(iv) your current profession and what you want to be in the future

____

____

____

____

____

____

____

____

____

____

____

____

____

____

(Do NOT write your real name and address, but include the date in Spanish and use the appropriate beginning and ending.)

Sección II Total = 30 Puntos

SECCIÓN III

EL DIÁLOGO CONTEXTUAL (CONTEXTUAL DIALOGUE)
LEE Y RELLENA EL DIÁLOGO EN ESPAÑOL
(READ AND COMPLETE THE DIALOGUE IN SPANISH)

ESPAÑA

BAILARINA DE FLAMENCO

PAELLA

3. **Use 40 – 50 words to complete the dialogue between you and your friend, Sandra, giving your responses in SPANISH.**

   Your Guatemalan friend, Sandra is interviewing you about your country for an article in her school magazine. Complete the dialogue you have with her on *Messenger.* Include:

   (i) greetings
   (ii) information about your country
   (iii) the leader of your country
   (iv) famous people from your country
   (v) response to thanks and bid goodbye

Responses to ALL the cues provided must be included in the completed dialogue.

Sandra: Hola, ¿qué tal?

Tú: ______________________________

Sandra: Estoy bien, gracias. ¿De dónde eres?

Tú: ______________________________

Sandra: Muy bien. ¿Y cuáles son los colores de tu país?

Tú: ______________________________

Sandra: ¡Qué colores bonitos! ¿Y cuál es la capital de tu país?

Tú: ______________________________

Sandra: ¿Quién es el primer ministro/ la primera ministra de tu país?

Tú: ______________________________

Sandra: ¿Quién es famoso/a en tu país?

Tú: ______________________________

Sandra: Bueno. Muchas gracias.

Tú: ______________________________

Sandra: Hasta luego.

Tú: ______________________________

CORRIDA DE TOROS (BULLFIGHTING)

Sección III Total = 20 Puntos

SECCIÓN IV

COMPRENSIÓN DE LECTURA (READING COMPREHENSION)
RESPONDE A CADA PREGUNTA (ANSWER ALL QUESTIONS)

4. **Lee la siguiente selección con cuidado y responde a las preguntas en INGLÉS.**

Read the following selection carefully. Do NOT translate but answer the questions in ENGLISH.

YOU WILL BE PENALIZED FOR DISREGARDING THESE INSTRUCTIONS.

Spanish Around the World

El español es la lengua* oficial de veintiún países. En el Caribe, Cuba, la República Dominicana y Puerto Rico son los países donde español es la lengua oficial. En América Central, seis países tienen español como* lengua oficial. Panamá, Nicaragua y El Salvador son países en América Central. En los continentes Europa y África solo* un país tiene español como lengua oficial: España en Europa y Guinea Ecuatorial en África.

En Sudamérica, nueve países tienen español como lengua oficial. Países como: Chile, Argentina, Perú y Bolivia. La lengua y la cultura española son interesantes. Machu Picchu es muy popular en Perú y Salar de Uyuni es muy famoso en Bolivia. También, Santiago, la capital de Chile es famoso. En 2020, 463 millones de personas son hablantes nativos de español. ¡Viva español!

(131 palabras)

***lengua – tongue/language**
***como – as/like**
*** solo – only**

Answer the questions in ENGLISH, based on the selection above.
Use a complete sentence for each response.

(a) How many countries have Spanish as an official language? **(1 punto)**

____

(b) What is said about the Caribbean? **(2 puntos)**

____

(c) Which Central American countries are named? **(3 puntos)**

____

(d) What does the passage say about Spain? **(2 puntos)**

____

(e) Which is the Spanish-speaking country in Africa? **(1 punto)**

____

(f) How many countries in Europe and Africa speak Spanish in total? **(2 puntos)**

____

(g) Which is the last continent mentioned? **(1 punto)**

____

(h) List THREE (3) Spanish-speaking countries on the last continent stated. **(3 puntos)**

____

(i) Name THREE (3) popular places in three Spanish-speaking countries. **(3 puntos)**

____

____

(j) What are described as interesting? **(2 puntos)**

____

Sección IV Total = 20 Puntos

TOTAL PUNTOS POR PRUEBA = 100

FIN DE PRUEBA (END OF TEST)

REVISA TU TRABAJO POR FAVOR (PLEASE CHECK YOUR WORK)

ESPAÑA

BAILARINA DE FLAMENCO

PAELLA

CORRIDA DE TOROS (BULLFIGHTING)

PAPEL ADICIONAL/NO FALTA NADA DE ESTA PÁGINA

(EXTRA PAPER)/(NOTHING IS MISSING FROM THIS PAGE)

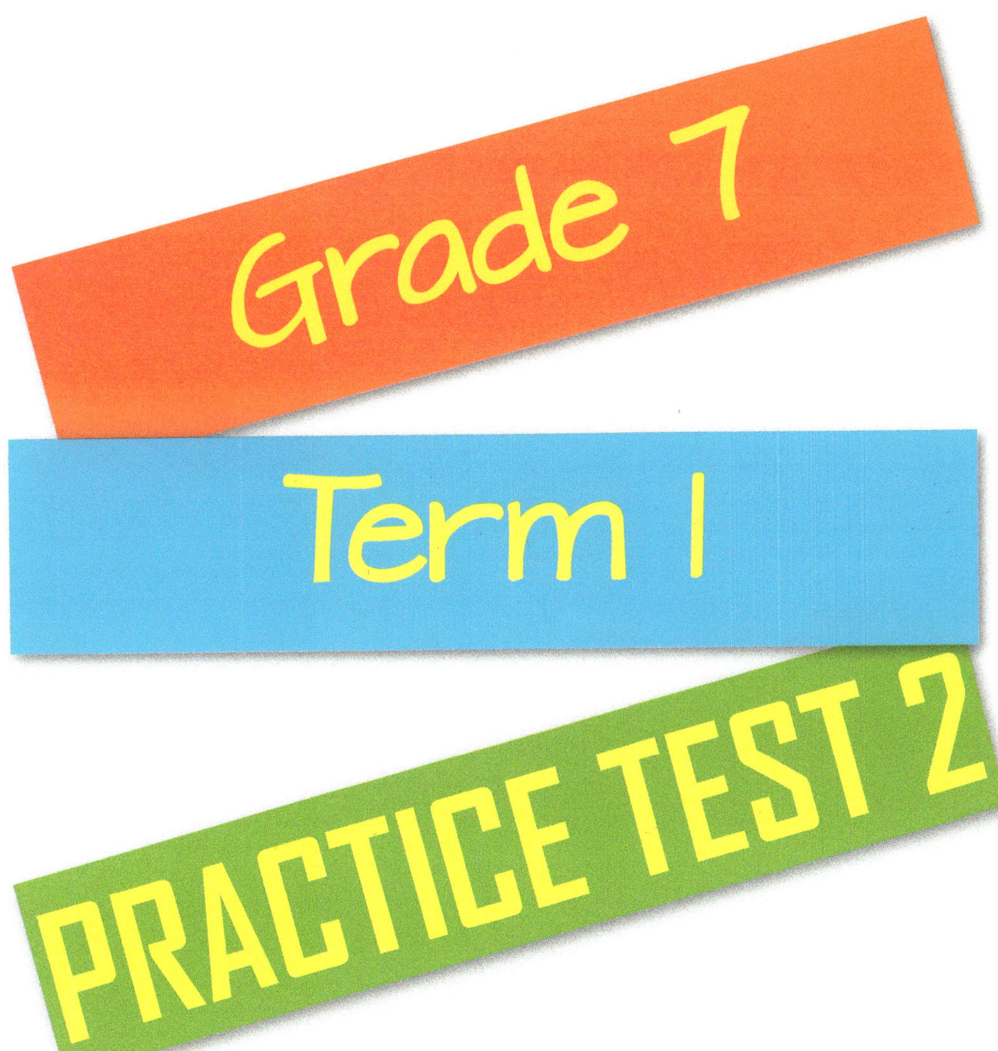

CUBA
(BIG PLACE / PLACE IN THE CENTRE)

CIGARROS CUBANOS
(CUBAN CIGARS)

COLIBRÍ DE ABEJA (BEE HUMMINGBIRD)

LA HABANA, CUBA

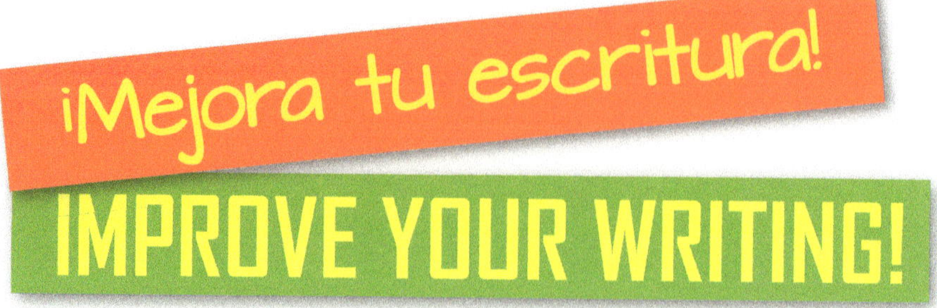

No cometas los mismos errores

(Don't make the same mistakes)

Below are common mistakes made by students of Spanish. Please note the mistakes and the corrections given. By avoiding these mistakes, you will be sure to improve your writing skills in Spanish.

PUNTUACIÓN Y MAYÚSCULAS (PUNCTUATION AND CAPITALIZATION)		
Inglés	Español con error	Español correcto
1. I am Trinidadian.	Soy Trinitense.	Soy trinitense.
2. Today is Monday.	Hoy es Lunes.	Hoy es lunes.
3. What is your name?	Cómo te llamas?	¿Cómo te llamas?
4. Silence please!	Silencio por favor!	¡Silencio por favor!
5. My birthday is on June 4.	Mi cumpleaños es el 4 de Junio.	Mi cumpleaños es el 4 de junio.

LETRAS CON TILDES (LETTERS WITH TILDES)		
Inglés	Español con error	Español correcto
1. How are you?	¿Como estas?	¿Cómo estás?
2. She is my mom/ mommy.	Ella es mi mama.	Ella es mi mamá.
3. Mr. Brown is kind.	El senor Brown es generoso.	El señor Brown es generoso.
4. Spanish is fun!	¡Espanol es divertido!	¡Español es divertido!
5. What is your nationality?	¿Cual es tu nacionalidad?	¿Cuál es tu nacionalidad?

EL VOCABULARIO (VOCABULARY)		
Inglés	Español con error	Español correcto
1. My birthday es on Friday.	Mi cumpleaños es en viernes.	Mi cumpleaños es el viernes.
2. The chocolate is large.	El chocolate es largo.	El chocolate es grande.
3. My parents are short.	Mis parientes son bajos.	Mis padres son bajos.
4. My cousin is short.	Me primo es bajo.	Mi primo es bajo.
5. You are brave.	Tu eres valiente.	Tú eres valiente.

Respuestas Abiertas (Free Response)

Nombre:______________________________ Apellido: ________________________

Clase:________________________________ Profesor/a: ______________________

Fecha: ____

Duración: 90 minutos

INSTRUCCIONES

1. **Esta prueba tiene CUATRO (4) secciones. Responde a cada pregunta en este papel.**

   This test has FOUR (4) sections. Answer all questions on this paper.

2. **Sección I: Tiene DIEZ (10) situaciones. Responde a cada situación en ESPAÑOL.**

   Section I: Has TEN (10) situations. Respond to each in SPANISH.

3. **Sección II: Tiene una carta informal. Escribe la carta en ESPAÑOL.**

   Section II: Has an informal letter. Write the letter in SPANISH.

4. **Sección III: Tiene un diálogo. Rellena los espacios en ESPAÑOL.**

   Section III: Has a dialogue. Complete the dialogue in SPANISH.

5. **Sección IV: Tiene una comprensión de lectura. Responde a las DIEZ (10) preguntas en INGLÉS.**

   Section IV: Has a reading comprehension. Answer the TEN (10) questions in ENGLISH.

SECCIÓN I

LAS SITUACIONES ESCRITAS (WRITTEN SITUATIONS)
RESPONDE A CADA SITUACIÓN (RESPOND TO EACH SITUATION)

1. **Write in SPANISH the information required by each of the situations given below. Do NOT write more than ONE sentence for each situation. For some situations, a complete sentence may not be necessary. Write each answer in the space provided.**

(a) You receive a beautiful gift from your new Cuban classmate. Write the thank-you note that you send him/her.

(3 puntos)

____

(b) Your Spanish teacher has asked each student to write the name and relation of any family member on a paper. What sentence do you write?

(3 puntos)

____

(c) You want to know how your Chilean friend is doing. What do you ask him/her in the *Facebook* message that you send?

(3 puntos)

____

(d) At your Argentinian friend's party, you are playing a game which requires each person to write something that he/she dislikes. What do you write?

(3 puntos)

____

(e) You ask your new friend from Uruguay to do something for you. What polite word(s) do you use at the end of your message?

(3 puntos)

____

(f) You are filling out a visa application form to visit Paraguay and one question asks your nationality. What do you write?

(3 puntos)

____

(g) In Spanish class, the teacher usually asks students to write the date on the board. He/she asks you to write the date. What do you write?

(3 puntos)

____

(h) It is a special day. What message do you send your Spanish-speaking relative?

(3 puntos)

____

(i) Your Panamanian friend wants to know about an item that you bought. Respond to the message mentioning its colour.

(3 puntos)

____

(j) You are going to bed. What is the final text message that you send to your classmate who speaks Spanish?

(3 puntos)

____

Sección I Total = 30 Puntos

CUBA
(BIG PLACE / PLACE IN THE CENTRE)

CIGARROS CUBANOS
(CUBAN CIGARS)

COLIBRÍ DE ABEJA
(BEE HUMMING BIRD)

LA HABANA, CUBA

LA CARTA INFORMAL (INFORMAL LETTER)
ESCRIBE UNA CARTA EN ESPAÑOL (WRITE A LETTER IN SPANISH)

2. Using the following outline as a guide, write a letter in SPANISH of no more than 40 – 50 words.

YOU WILL BE PENALIZED FOR DISREGARDING THESE INSTRUCTIONS.

You enter a Spanish letter writing contest at the embassy of Spain in your country. You are required to write a friendly letter about your family. Include:

(i) your name, and the number of persons in your family

(ii) the names and description of any TWO (2) family members

(iii) the profession of any TWO (2) family members

(iv) your favourite family member

(Do NOT write your real name and address, but include the date in Spanish and use the appropriate beginning and ending.)

Sección II Total = 30 Puntos

SECCIÓN III

EL DIÁLOGO CONTEXTUAL (CONTEXTUAL DIALOGUE)
LEE Y RELLENA EL DIÁLOGO EN ESPAÑOL
(READ AND COMPLETE THE DIALOGUE IN SPANISH)

CUBA
(BIG PLACE / PLACE IN THE CENTRE)

3. Use 40 – 50 words to complete the dialogue between you and the local newspaper (Noticiero Local), giving your responses in SPANISH.

It's *International Day of Friendship* and the local newspaper has a competition for students studying Spanish. You can win a prize if you answer the questions about your best friend correctly. Email your answers. Include:

(i) your name
(ii) information about your friend
(iii) what your friend likes
(iv) your friend's favourite colour
(v) response to thanks and bid goodbye

CIGARROS CUBANOS
(CUBAN CIGARS)

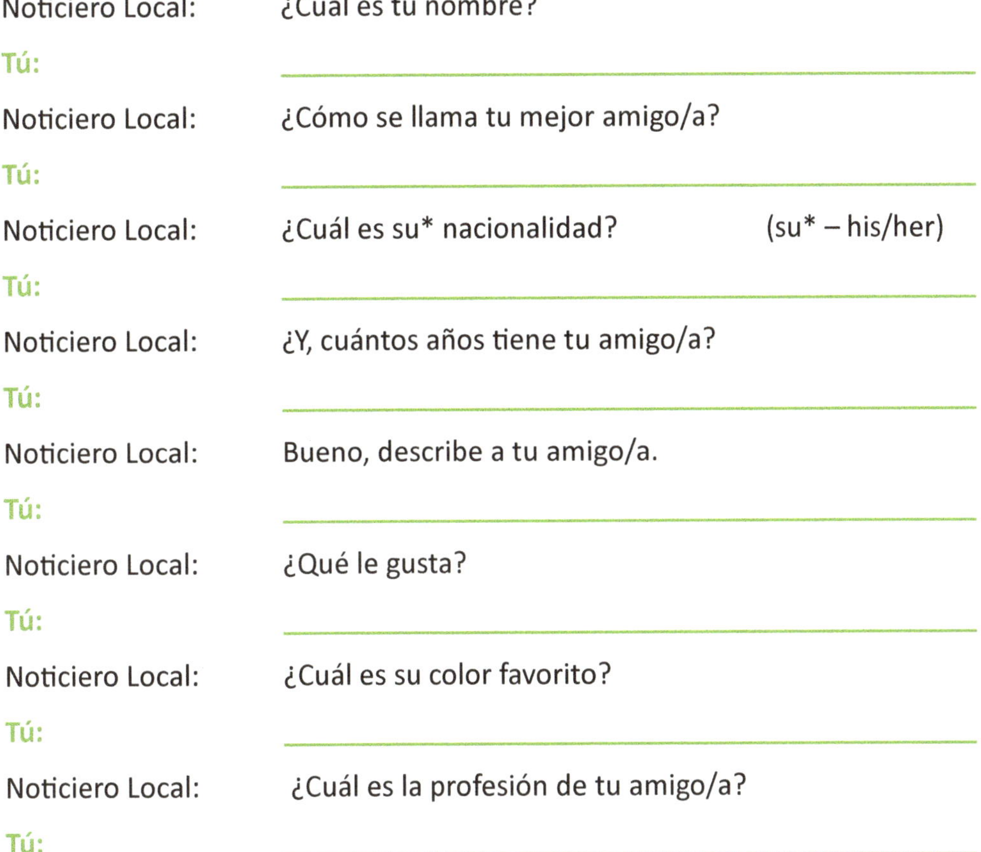

Responses to ALL the cues provided must be included in the completed dialogue.

Noticiero Local: ¿Cuál es tu nombre?

Tú: ______________________________

Noticiero Local: ¿Cómo se llama tu mejor amigo/a?

Tú: ______________________________

Noticiero Local: ¿Cuál es su* nacionalidad? (su* – his/her)

Tú: ______________________________

Noticiero Local: ¿Y, cuántos años tiene tu amigo/a?

Tú: ______________________________

Noticiero Local: Bueno, describe a tu amigo/a.

Tú: ______________________________

Noticiero Local: ¿Qué le gusta?

Tú: ______________________________

Noticiero Local: ¿Cuál es su color favorito?

Tú: ______________________________

Noticiero Local: ¿Cuál es la profesión de tu amigo/a?

Tú: ______________________________

COLIBRÍ DE ABEJA
(BEE HUMMING BIRD)

LA HABANA, CUBA

Sección III Total = 20 Puntos

El Caribe

Cada país tiene una cultura diferente y única.

SECCIÓN IV

COMPRENSIÓN DE LECTURA (READING COMPREHENSION)
RESPONDE A CADA PREGUNTA (ANSWER ALL QUESTIONS)

4. Lee la siguiente selección con cuidado y responde a las preguntas en INGLÉS.

Read the following selection carefully. Do NOT translate but answer the questions in ENGLISH.

YOU WILL BE PENALIZED FOR DISREGARDING THESE INSTRUCTIONS.

Caribbean People: Gifted and Strong

El Caribe es un grupo de islas en el mar* caribeño. Hay muchos países en el Caribe. En total, hay veintiséis. La cultura en cada país es diferente y única*. Por ejemplo, la cultura en Haití es diferente de la cultura de Cuba y de San Vicente y las Granadinas. La cultura de Haití tiene influencia de Francia, la cultura de Cuba tiene influencia de España y la cultura de San Vicente tiene influencia de Inglaterra. Muchos de los países tienen influencias de África también. Las personas del Caribe son talentosas, creativas y fuertes.

Las personas caribeñas son talentosas. Por ejemplo, hay Rihanna, la cantante de Barbados, Curtly Ambrose, el jugador de críquet de Antigua y Barbuda, y el atleta Kirani James de Granada. Hay muchas artistas, autores y atletas en la región ¡Tú, también, eres talentoso/a y fuerte!

(139 palabras)

***el mar – sea**
*** única/o – unique**

Answer the questions in ENGLISH, based on the selection above.
Use a complete sentence for each response.

(a) Where are the Caribbean islands located? **(1 punto)**

____

(b) How many countries are there in the Caribbean? **(1 punto)**

____

(c) How is the culture of Caribbean countries described? **(2 puntos)**

____

(d) What countries influence Haiti's and Cuba's culture? **(2 puntos)**

____

(e) What is said about Saint Vincent? **(2 puntos)**

____

(f) What does the passage say about Africa? **(2 puntos)**

____

(g) Give THREE (3) descriptions of Caribbean people **(3 puntos)**

____

(h) What is said about Rihanna? **(2 puntos)**

____

(i) Who is Curtly Ambrose? **(2 puntos)**

____

(j) Give any THREE (3) professions mentioned. **(3 puntos)**

____

Sección IV Total = 20 Puntos

TOTAL PUNTOS POR PRUEBA = 100
FIN DE PRUEBA (END OF TEST)
REVISA TU TRABAJO POR FAVOR (PLEASE CHECK YOUR WORK)

CUBA
(BIG PLACE / PLACE IN THE CENTRE)

CIGARROS CUBANOS
(CUBAN CIGARS)

COLIBRÍ DE ABEJA
(BEE HUMMING BIRD)

LA HABANA, CUBA

PAPEL ADICIONAL/NO FALTA NADA DE ESTA PÁGINA

(EXTRA PAPER)/(NOTHING IS MISSING FROM THIS PAGE)

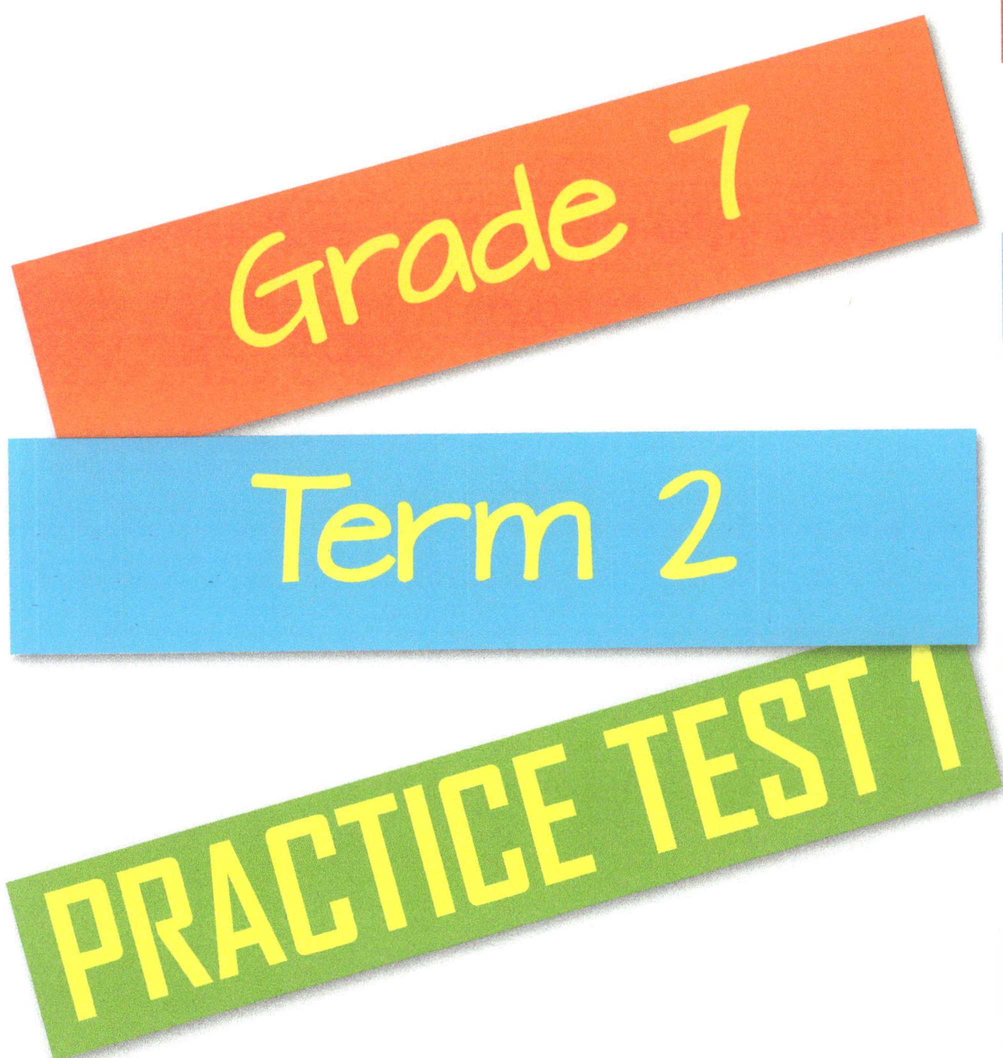

POZO PETROLÍFERO (OIL WELL)

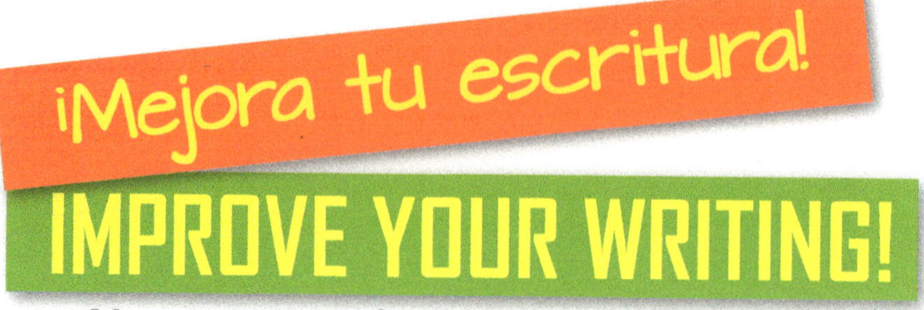

No cometas los mismos errores

(Don't make the same mistakes)

Below are common mistakes made by students of Spanish. Please note the mistakes and the corrections given. By avoiding these mistakes, you will be sure to improve your writing skills in Spanish.

LA GRAMÁTICA (GRAMMAR)		
Inglés	Español con error	Español correcto
1. The class is at 2 p.m.	La clase es a son las dos de la tarde.	La clase es a las dos de la tarde.
2. It is sunny.	Es sol.	Hace sol.
3. Marcos has two pens.	Marcos tienes dos plumas.	Marcos tiene dos plumas.
4. There are two erasers.	Hay dos borrador.	Hay dos borradores.
5. I have a map.	Tengo una mapa.	Tengo un mapa.

LA ORTOGRAFÍA (SPELLING)		
Inglés	Español con error	Español correcto
1. There are many animals.	Hay muchos animals.	Hay muchos animales.
2. Happy birthday!	¡Felix cumpleaños!	¡Feliz cumpleaños!
3. Do you like fruits?	¿Te gustan las fruitas?	¿Te gustan las frutas?
4. My school is called...	Mi escuela se yama...	Mi escuela se llama...
5. There are thirty chairs in the class.	Hay trienta sillas en la clase.	Hay treinta sillas en la clase.

EL ORDEN DE LAS PALABRAS (WORD ORDER)		
Inglés	Español con error	Español correcto
1. Where do you live?	¿Dónde tú vives?	¿Dónde vives tú?
2. The dog is my favourite animal.	El perro es mi favorito animal.	El perro es mi animal favorito.
3. I don't like art.	Me no gusta el arte.	No me gusta el arte.
4. She has a yellow book.	Ella tiene un amarillo libro.	Ella tiene un libro amarillo.

Respuestas Abiertas (Free Response)

Nombre:__________________________ Apellido: ______________________

Clase:____________________________ Profesor/a: ____________________

Fecha: ____

Duración: 90 minutos

INSTRUCCIONES

1. **Esta prueba tiene CUATRO (4) secciones. Responde a cada pregunta en este papel.**

   This test has FOUR (4) sections. Answer all questions on this paper.

2. **Sección I: Tiene DIEZ (10) situaciones. Responde a cada situación en ESPAÑOL.**

   Section I: Has TEN (10) situations. Respond to each in SPANISH.

3. **Sección II: Tiene una carta informal. Escribe la carta en ESPAÑOL.**

   Section II: Has an informal letter. Write the letter in SPANISH.

4. **Sección III: Tiene un diálogo. Rellena los espacios en ESPAÑOL.**

   Section III: Has a dialogue. Complete the dialogue in SPANISH.

5. **Sección IV: Tiene una comprensión de lectura. Responde a las DIEZ (10) preguntas en INGLÉS.**

   Section IV: Has a reading comprehension. Answer the TEN (10) questions in ENGLISH.

España

SECCIÓN I

LAS SITUACIONES ESCRITAS (WRITTEN SITUATIONS)
RESPONDE A CADA SITUACIÓN (RESPOND TO EACH SITUATION)

1. **Write in SPANISH the information required by each of the situations given below. Do NOT write more than ONE sentence for each situation. For some situations, a complete sentence may not be necessary. Write each answer in the space provided.**

   (a) Your Venezuelan friend has stopped to buy fruits and sends you a message asking you your favourite fruit. What do you reply in the text message?

   (3 puntos)

   ____

   (b) You are attending a new school and your Spanish-speaking friend asks you the colour of your classroom. What do you reply online?

   (3 puntos)

   ____

   (c) Your Salvadorian friend messages you and asks if you like your school. What do you reply in your text to him/her?

   (3 puntos)

   ____

   (d) At a Spanish club meeting, your teacher tells you to describe yourself on your nametag. What do you write?

   (3 puntos)

   ____

   (e) Your Puerto Rican friend is upset with you because of something you did. Send a message of apology to him/her.

   (3 puntos)

   ____

(f) A new student has joined your Spanish class. Write the welcome note that you send to him/her.

(3 puntos)

____

(g) It is 3 p.m. Send your Peruvian friend a text message greeting him/her.

(3 puntos)

____

(h) You won a gold medal at the Spanish festival. What does your Spanish teacher say to you in the message that he/she sends you?

(3 puntos)

____

(i) Your cousin who loves Spanish wants to know which days of the week you have Spanish classes. What message do you send him/her on *WhatsApp*?

(3 puntos)

____

(j) Your Bolivian pen pal has written you to ask where in your country you live. What do you reply?

(3 puntos)

____

Sección I Total = 30 Puntos

VENEZUELA (LITTLE VENICE)

SIMÓN BOLÍVAR

AREPA

POZO PETROLÍFERO (OIL WELL)

SECCIÓN II

LA CARTA INFORMAL (INFORMAL LETTER)
ESCRIBE UNA CARTA EN ESPAÑOL (WRITE A LETTER IN SPANISH)

2. Using the following outline as a guide, write a letter in SPANISH of no more than 40 – 50 words.

YOU WILL BE PENALIZED FOR DISREGARDING THESE INSTRUCTIONS.

This is your first year in high school. Write a letter to your Colombian friend giving him/her basic information about your school. Include:

(i) the name of your school and its colours

(ii) the number of students in your class

(iii) a description of any TWO (2) of your teachers

(iv) any subjects that you like and dislike

____

____

____

____

____

____

____

____

____

____

____

____

____

____

(Do NOT write your real name and address, but include the date in Spanish and use the appropriate beginning and ending.)

Sección II Total = 30 Puntos

SECCIÓN III

EL DIÁLOGO CONTEXTUAL (CONTEXTUAL DIALOGUE)
LEE Y RELLENA EL DIÁLOGO EN ESPAÑOL
(READ AND COMPLETE THE DIALOGUE IN SPANISH)

3. **Use 40 – 50 words to complete the dialogue between you and a representative from a fruit company, giving your responses in SPANISH.**

   You enter a competition for a chance to win free fruits for a year. You have a brief conversation over *WhatsApp* with a Mexican representative from the fruit company. Answer the questions by including:

   (i) greetings and wellbeing (how you're doing)
   (ii) your favourite fruit
   (iii) popular fruits in your country
   (iv) information about fruit salads that you eat
   (v) a response to thanks and bid goodbye

Responses to ALL the cues provided must be included in the completed dialogue.

Representante: ¡Hola! Buenos días. ¿Cómo estás?

Tú: ______________________________

Representante: Bueno. ¿Cuál es tu fruta favorita?

Tú: ______________________________

Representante: ¿Cuáles son los colores de tu fruta favorita?

Tú: ______________________________

Representante: Y, ¿cuáles te gustan más: las uvas o las fresas?

Tú: ______________________________

Representante: Bien. ¿Qué frutas son populares en tu país?

Tú: ______________________________

Representante: ¿Cuáles son los colores de las manzanas en tu país?

Tú: ______________________________

Representante: ¿Cuántas frutas te gustan en tu ensalada* de frutas? (*ensalada –salad)

Tú: ______________________________

Representante: Muchas gracias. Chao.

Tú: ______________________________

Sección III Total = 20 Puntos

VENEZUELA (LITTLE VENICE)

SIMÓN BOLÍVAR

AREPA

POZO PETROLÍFERO (OIL WELL)

Cuba

SECCIÓN IV

COMPRENSIÓN DE LECTURA (READING COMPREHENSION)
RESPONDE A CADA PREGUNTA (ANSWER ALL QUESTIONS)

4. Lee la siguiente selección con cuidado y responde a las preguntas en INGLÉS.

Read the following selection carefully. Do NOT translate but answer the questions in ENGLISH.

YOU WILL BE PENALIZED FOR DISREGARDING THESE INSTRUCTIONS.

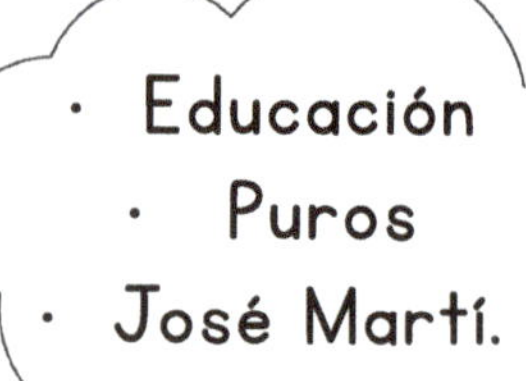

Cuba

Cuba es una isla en el Caribe. La capital de Cuba es la Habana. La isla tiene más de once millones de personas y español es la lengua oficial del país. En el año 1492, Cristóbal Colón fue* a Cuba. La isla se llama,"la perla del Caribe". La música "rumba" es muy popular en Cuba. La educación es muy importante a los cubanos. En las escuelas en Cuba muchas clases tienen quince estudiantes. Las clases son pequeñas. El béisbol es el deporte número uno en Cuba. El basquetbol es popular también.

Unos cubanos famosos son Fidel Castro (ex presidente), Gloria Estefan (cantante), Javier Sotomayor (ex atleta) y José Martí (héroe nacional de Cuba, ex poeta y ex profesor). Cuba es un país hermoso.

(125 palabras)

***fue – went**

Answer the questions in ENGLISH, based on the selection above. Use a complete sentence for each response.

(a) What is the capital city of Cuba? **(1 punto)**

____

(b) How many people live in Cuba? **(2 puntos)**

____

(c) What is said about Christopher Columbus? **(2 puntos)**

____

(d) What is Cuba sometimes called? **(2 puntos)**

____

(e) What does the passage say about "rumba"? **(2 puntos)**

____

(f) According to the passage, what is important to Cubans? **(1 punto)**

____

(g) Describe class sizes in some schools in Cuba. **(2 puntos)**

____

(h) What sports are mentioned? **(2 puntos)**

____

(i) Name three (3) famous Cubans. **(3 puntos)**

____

(j) Who was José Martí? **(3 puntos)**

____

Sección IV Total = 20 Puntos

TOTAL PUNTOS POR PRUEBA = 100
FIN DE PRUEBA (END OF TEST)
REVISA TU TRABAJO POR FAVOR (PLEASE CHECK YOUR WORK)

VENEZUELA (LITTLE VENICE)

SIMÓN BOLÍVAR

AREPA

POZO PETROLÍFERO (OIL WELL)

PAPEL ADICIONAL/NO FALTA NADA DE ESTA PÁGINA

(EXTRA PAPER)/(NOTHING IS MISSING FROM THIS PAGE)

MÉXICO / MÉJICO
(IN THE NAVEL OF THE MOON)

Grade 7

Term 2

PRACTICE TEST 2

TACO

GUITARRÓN MEXICANO
(MEXICAN GUITAR)

SOMBRERO

No cometas los mismos errores
(Don't make the same mistakes)

Below are common mistakes made by students of Spanish. Please note the mistakes and the corrections given. By avoiding these mistakes, you will be sure to improve your writing skills in Spanish.

PUNTUACIÓN Y MAYÚSCULAS (PUNCTUATION AND CAPITALIZATION)		
Inglés	Español con error	Español correcto
1. It is the 4th of July.	Es el 4 de Julio.	Es el 4 de julio.
2. Mr. Brown is honest.	El Señor Brown es honesto.	El señor Brown es honesto.
3. When is your birthday?	Cuándo es tu cumpleaños?	¿Cuándo es tu cumpleaños?
4. Sit, please!	Siéntense, por favor!	¡Siéntense, por favor!
5. I like Spanish.	Me gusta Español.	Me gusta español.

LETRAS CON TILDES (LETTERS WITH TILDES)		
Inglés	Español con error	Español correcto
1. Tomorrow is Sunday.	Manana es domingo.	Mañana es domingo.
2. Do you have my pencil?	¿Tienes mi lapiz?	¿Tienes mi lápiz?
3. It's raining.	Esta lloviendo.	Está lloviendo.
4. The pineapple is sweet.	La pina es dulce.	La piña es dulce.
5. What is your address?	¿Cuál es tu direccíon?	¿Cuál es tu dirección?

EL VOCABULARIO (VOCABULARY)		
Inglés	Español con error	Español correcto
1. I like grapes.	Me gustan las grapas.	Me gustan las uvas.
2. The dog is big.	El pero es grande.	El perro es grande.
3. We have many chairs.	Tenemos muy sillas.	Tenemos muchas sillas.
4. Ms. Smith, you are strong.	Señorita Smith, tú eres fuerte.	Señorita Smith, usted es fuerte.
5. The ruler is long.	La regular es larga.	La regla es larga.

Respuestas Abiertas (Free Response)

Nombre:____________________________ Apellido: ________________________

Clase:______________________________ Profesor/a: ______________________

Fecha: ____

Duración: 90 minutos

INSTRUCCIONES

1. **Esta prueba tiene CUATRO (4) secciones. Responde a cada pregunta en este papel.**

   This test has FOUR (4) sections. Answer all questions on this paper.

2. **Sección I: Tiene DIEZ (10) situaciones. Responde a cada situación en ESPAÑOL.**

   Section I: Has TEN (10) situations. Respond to each in SPANISH.

3. **Sección II: Tiene una carta informal. Escribe la carta en ESPAÑOL.**

   Section II: Has an informal letter. Write the letter in SPANISH.

4. **Sección III: Tiene un diálogo. Rellena los espacios en ESPAÑOL.**

   Section III: Has a dialogue. Complete the dialogue in SPANISH.

5. **Sección IV: Tiene una comprensión de lectura. Responde a las DIEZ (10) preguntas en INGLÉS.**

   Section IV: Has a reading comprehension. Answer the TEN (10) questions in ENGLISH.

Colombia

SECCIÓN I

LAS SITUACIONES ESCRITAS (WRITTEN SITUATIONS)
RESPONDE A CADA SITUACIÓN (RESPOND TO EACH SITUATION)

1. Write in SPANISH the information required by each of the situations given below. Do NOT write more than ONE sentence for each situation. For some situations, a complete sentence may not be necessary. Write each answer in the space provided.

(a) Your new *Instagram* friend from Spain has sent you a message asking you the time in your country. What do you reply?

(3 puntos)

____

(b) You are filling out an application form for a visa to go to Mexico for the summer. One of the questions asks your date of birth. What do you write?

(3 puntos)

____

(c) Your friend from Panama has just bought a pet dog and sends you a message asking what animal you like. What do you reply?

(3 puntos)

____

(d) You receive a message on *Facebook Messenger* from your Spanish-speaking friend asking you how many siblings you have. How do you reply?

(3 puntos)

____

(e) At a conference for students studying Spanish, you are asked to write a stationery item you want as a present at the end of the conference. Which one do you write?

(3 puntos)

____

(f) Your pen pal from the Dominican Republic has sent you a picture of himself/herself collecting a trophy. Send him/her a message of congratulations.

(3 puntos)

____

(g) You did something special for your teacher of Spanish on Teachers' Day. He/she sends you a message thanking you. What do you reply?

(3 puntos)

____

(h) Your Puerto Rican friend asks how long one of your Spanish classes lasts. What do you reply in the text message that you send?

(3 puntos)

____

(i) There is a visitor at your school and your Spanish teacher has asked each student to write a question for the visitor. What question do you write?

(3 puntos)

____

(j) Your Bolivian friend asks you what the weather is like in your country. What do you reply in the message that you send?

(3 puntos)

____

Sección I Total = 30 Puntos

SECCIÓN II

LA CARTA INFORMAL (INFORMAL LETTER)
ESCRIBE UNA CARTA EN ESPAÑOL (WRITE A LETTER IN SPANISH)

2. Using the following outline as a guide, write a letter in SPANISH of no more than 40 – 50 words.

YOU WILL BE PENALIZED FOR DISREGARDING THESE INSTRUCTIONS.

There are many famous persons in your country. Write a letter to your friend from Equatorial Guinea in Africa about a famous person in your country. Include:

(i) the name and nationality of the person

(ii) a description of the person

(iii) the person's profession/job

(iv) why you like the person

____

____

____

____

____

____

____

____

____

____

____

____

____

____

(Do NOT write your real name and address, but include the date in Spanish and use the appropriate beginning and ending.)

Sección II Total = 30 Puntos

SECCIÓN III

EL DIÁLOGO CONTEXTUAL (CONTEXTUAL DIALOGUE)
LEE Y RELLENA EL DIÁLOGO EN ESPAÑOL
(READ AND COMPLETE THE DIALOGUE IN SPANISH)

3. **Use 40 – 50 words to complete the dialogue between you and an animal lover, giving your responses in SPANISH.**

   You recently went to the zoo and posted a picture of animals on *Instagram*. Your Spanish-speaking friend begins a conversation with you online about animals. Respond to him/her by including:

   (i) greetings and wellbeing
   (ii) popular animals in your country
   (iii) whether you have pets or not
   (iv) animals at the zoo
   (v) goodbye

Responses to ALL the cues provided must be included in the completed dialogue.

Amigo/a: Hola. ¡Qué foto bonita! ¿Qué tal?

Tú: ____________________

Amigo/a: ¿Hay elefantes en tu país?

Tú: ____________________

Amigo/a: ¿Qué animales son populares en tu país?

Tú: ____________________

Amigo/a: ¡Interesante! ¿Tienes animales domésticos?

Tú: ____________________

Amigo/a: Bien. ¿Te gustan los animales grandes o pequeños?

Tú: ____________________

Amigo/a: ¿De qué colores son los perros en tu país?

Tú: ____________________

Amigo/a: ¿Qué animales hay en el zoo?

Tú: ____________________

Amigo/a: ¡Bueno! En mi país también. Gracias y hasta luego.

Tú: ____________________

Sección III Total = 20 Puntos

Chile

SECCIÓN IV

COMPRENSIÓN DE LECTURA (READING COMPREHENSION)
RESPONDE A CADA PREGUNTA (ANSWER ALL QUESTIONS)

4. Lee la siguiente selección con cuidado y responde a las preguntas en INGLÉS.

Read the following selection carefully. Do NOT translate but answer the questions in ENGLISH.

YOU WILL BE PENALIZED FOR DISREGARDING THESE INSTRUCTIONS.

Anguilla: Made for You

Anguila es una isla pequeña que está al este del Caribe. La isla tiene este nombre porque tiene la forma* de un pez-serpiente largo y flaco. Al sur de Anguila está la isla de San Cristóbal y Nieves y al oeste está la isla de Puerto Rico. La lengua oficial de Puerto Rico es español pero en Anguila, es inglés.

La capital de Anguila se llama 'El Valle'. Los vegetales y el tabaco son populares en el país. A los actores como Sandra Bullock, Liam Neeson y Chuck Norris les gusta Anguila. No hay ríos en Anguilla pero hay treinta y tres playas*. Normalmente hace sol en el país. Hay seis escuelas primarias públicas y una escuela secundaria pública en Anguila.

(119 palabras)

la forma* – shape
las playas* – beaches

Answer the questions in ENGLISH, based on the selection above. Use a complete sentence for each response.

(a) Describe Anguilla. **(1 punto)**

____

(b) Where is Anguilla located? **(2 puntos)**

____

(c) Why does the island have that name? (3 puntos)

___

(d) Which countries are to the South and West of Anguilla? (2 puntos)

___

(e) What are the official languages of Anguilla and Puerto Rico? (2 puntos)

___

(f) What is the capital of Anguilla? (1 punto)

___

(g) Which crops are grown in Anguilla? (2 puntos)

___

(h) Which celebrities have visited Anguilla? (3 puntos)

___

(i) How many rivers and beaches are in Anguilla? (2 puntos)

___

(j) What is said about high school in Anguilla? (2 puntos)

___

Sección IV Total = 20 Puntos

TOTAL PUNTOS POR PRUEBA = 100
FIN DE PRUEBA (END OF TEST)
REVISA TU TRABAJO POR FAVOR (PLEASE CHECK YOUR WORK)

PAPEL ADICIONAL/NO FALTA NADA DE ESTA PÁGINA

(EXTRA PAPER)/(NOTHING IS MISSING FROM THIS PAGE)

Grade 7

Term 3

PRACTICE TEST 1

HONDURAS
(DEPTHS)

LAS BANANAS (BANANAS)

RUINAS DE COPÁN

LA GUACAMAYA ROJA
(SCARLET MACAU)

No cometas los mismos errores
(Don't make the same mistakes)

Below are common mistakes made by students of Spanish. Please note the mistakes and the corrections given. By avoiding these mistakes, you will be sure to improve your writing skills in Spanish.

LA GRAMÁTICA (GRAMMAR)		
Inglés	Español con error	Español correcto
1. The book is in the class.	El libro es en la clase.	El libro está en la clase.
2. Summer is one of the four seasons.	El verano es uno de las cuatro estaciones.	El verano es una de las cuatro estaciones.
3. The boy wears a T-shirt.	El niño llevo una camiseta.	El niño lleva una camiseta.
4. There are four chairs under the table.	Hay cuatro silla debajo de la mesa.	Hay cuatro sillas debajo de la mesa.
5. My house has two bedrooms.	Mi casa hay dos dormitorios.	Mi casa tiene dos dormitorios.

LA ORTOGRAFÍA (SPELLING)		
Inglés	Español con error	Español correcto
1. I like clothes.	Me gustan las ropas.	Me gusta la ropa.
2. Her pants are beautiful.	Sus pantilones son bonitos.	Sus pantalones son bonitos.
3. There are six rooms.	Hay sies habitaciones.	Hay seis habitaciones.
4. This book is excellent.	Éste libro es excellente.	Este libro es excelente.
5. My kitchen has a fridge.	Mi cosina tiene una nevera.	Mi cocina tiene una nevera.

EL ORDEN DE LAS PALABRAS (WORD ORDER)		
Inglés	Español con error	Español correcto
1. My house is not small.	Mi casa es no pequeña.	Mi casa no es pequeña.
2. She wears a pink blouse.	Ella lleva una rosada blusa.	Ella lleva una blusa rosada.
3. What are you wearing?	¿Qué tú llevas?	¿Qué llevas tú?
4. There is an old television.	Hay una vieja televisor.	Hay una televisor vieja.

Respuestas Abiertas (Free Response)

Nombre:______________________________ Apellido: ________________________

Clase:________________________________ Profesor/a: ______________________

Fecha: ____

Duración: 90 minutos

INSTRUCCIONES

1. **Esta prueba tiene CUATRO (4) secciones. Responde a cada pregunta en este papel.**

   This test has FOUR (4) sections. Answer all questions on this paper.

2. **Sección I: Tiene DIEZ (10) situaciones. Responde a cada situación en ESPAÑOL.**

   Section I: Has TEN (10) situations. Respond to each in SPANISH.

3. **Sección II: Tiene una carta informal. Escribe la carta en ESPAÑOL.**

   Section II: Has an informal letter. Write the letter in SPANISH.

4. **Sección III: Tiene un diálogo. Rellena los espacios en ESPAÑOL.**

   Section III: Has a dialogue. Complete the dialogue in SPANISH.

5. **Sección IV: Tiene una comprensión de lectura. Responde a las DIEZ (10) preguntas en INGLÉS.**

   Section IV: Has a reading comprehension. Answer the TEN (10) questions in ENGLISH.

Puerto Rico

· Mofongo

SECCIÓN I

LAS SITUACIONES ESCRITAS (WRITTEN SITUATIONS)
RESPONDE A CADA SITUACIÓN (RESPOND TO EACH SITUATION)

1. **Write in SPANISH the information required by each of the situations given below. Do NOT write more than ONE sentence for each situation. For some situations, a complete sentence may not be necessary. Write each answer in the space provided.**

(a) Your Uruguayan friend wants to know what time your school starts. What do you reply in the email that you send?

(3 puntos)

____

(b) You are at a party and your Nicaraguan neighbour enters wearing a beautiful outfit. What do you text him/her?

(3 puntos)

____

(c) You are creating a poster for Spanish day. What date do you write on it?

(3 puntos)

____

(d) The new Hispanic student in your class wants to know how many stationery items you have. What do you reply in the note you send back to him/her?

(3 puntos)

____

(e) Your Honduran friend is returning to his/her country. What do you write in the card you give him/her?

(3 puntos)

____

(f) Your Spanish-speaking friend from another country wants to know something about your classroom. What information do you provide on *Twitter*?

(3 puntos)

____

(g) You want to know if your Nicaraguan friend likes a particular subject. What do you ask in the message you send on *Instagram*?

(3 puntos)

____

(h) You receive a text message in Spanish asking you about one of your friends. What do you reply mentioning the friend's name?

(3 puntos)

____

(i) Your Mexican friend is visiting your island and sends you an email message asking you where you are. What do you reply?

(3 puntos)

____

(j) At a Spanish conference for grade seven students, everyone is asked to write something positive about himself/herself. What do you write?

(3 puntos)

____

Sección I Total = 30 Puntos

SECCIÓN II

LA CARTA INFORMAL (INFORMAL LETTER)
ESCRIBE UNA CARTA EN ESPAÑOL (WRITE A LETTER IN SPANISH)

2. Using the following outline as a guide, write a letter in SPANISH of no more than 40 – 50 words.

YOU WILL BE PENALIZED FOR DISREGARDING THESE INSTRUCTIONS.

It is *World Book Day (April 23)*. Write a letter to your Hispanic friend telling him/her about your favourite book. Include:

(i) the name of your favourite book

(ii) the author of your favourite book

(iii) a description of the book

(iv) the names of some persons/characters in the book

(Do NOT write your real name and address, but include the date in Spanish and use the appropriate beginning and ending.)

Sección II Total = 30 Puntos

SECCIÓN III

EL DIÁLOGO CONTEXTUAL (CONTEXTUAL DIALOGUE)
LEE Y RELLENA EL DIÁLOGO EN ESPAÑOL
(READ AND COMPLETE THE DIALOGUE IN SPANISH)

3. Use 40 – 50 words to complete the dialogue between you and an interviewer, giving your responses in SPANISH.

You are entering a weather competition and you have an online interview with a Spanish interviewer. Complete the interview by including:

(i) where you're from
(ii) summer weather conditions in your country
(iii) what you wear in the summer
(iv) your favourite season
(v) the rainiest months

Responses to ALL the cues provided must be included in the completed dialogue.

Entrevistador/a: Buenos días. ¿De dónde eres?

Tú: ______________________________

Entrevistador/a: ¿Qué tiempo hace durante el verano en tu país?

Tú: ______________________________

Entrevistador/a: ¿Qué llevas en el verano?

Tú: ______________________________

Entrevistador/a: ¡Yo también! ¿Te gusta el calor o el frío?

Tú: ______________________________

Entrevistador/a: Bueno. ¿Cuál es tu estación favorita?

Tú: ______________________________

Entrevistador/a: ¿En qué meses hay mucha lluvia en tu país? (la lluvia-rain)

Tú: ______________________________

Entrevistador/a: ¿Hace frío por la noche en tu país?

Tú: ______________________________

Entrevistador/a: Muchas gracias por la información. Adiós.

Tú: ______________________________

Sección III Total = 20 Puntos

HONDURAS (DEPTHS)
LAS BANANAS (BANANAS)
RUINAS DE COPÁN
LA GUACAMAYA ROJA (SCARLET MACAU)

Perú

SECCIÓN IV

COMPRENSIÓN DE LECTURA (READING COMPREHENSION)
RESPONDE A CADA PREGUNTA (ANSWER ALL QUESTIONS)

4. **Lee la siguiente selección con cuidado y responde a las preguntas en INGLÉS.**

Read the following selection carefully. Do NOT translate but answer the questions in ENGLISH.

YOU WILL BE PENALIZED FOR DISREGARDING THESE INSTRUCTIONS.

Grenadian Chocolate

Granada, también se llama 'la isla de especia*' o 'la capital caribeña de chocolate', es un país bonito. El cacao y el chocolate son muy populares en Granada y en el Caribe. Hay cuatro compañías grandes de chocolate en Granada. Por ejemplo hay, Jouvay, Crayfish Bay, La Compañía de Chocolate de Granada y Belmont Estate. El chocolate de cada compañia es muy delicioso y adictivo. Mott Green, Edmond Brown y Doug Brown son nombres famosos en La Compañía de Chocolate de Granada.

Cada año, en el mes de mayo, hay el festival de chocolate en Granada. El festival es por nueve días. En el país, también hay un mini museo de chocolate. El museo se llama 'Casa de Chocolate' y allí* tienen información sobre la historia del cacao y el chocolate en Granada. Hoy, Granada tiene unos de los mejores* chocolates en el mundo.

(144 palabras)

***la especia – spice**
***allí – there**
***los mejores – best**

Answer the questions in ENGLISH, based on the selection above. Use a complete sentence for each response.

(a) What names are given to Grenada? **(2 puntos)**

____

(b) What is Grenada famous for around the Caribbean? **(2 puntos)**

____

(c) What word is used to describe Grenada? (1 punto)

____

(d) Name THREE (3) famous companies mentioned. (3 puntos)

____

(e) Describe the companies' products. (2 puntos)

____

(f) Who are the famous Grenadians mentioned? (3 puntos)

____

____

(g) When is the festival mentioned, held in Grenada? (2 puntos)

____

(h) How long does the festival last? (1 punto)

____

(i) What can be found in the museum? (2 puntos)

____

(j) How is Grenadian chocolate described internationally? (2 puntos)

____

Sección IV Total = 20 Puntos

TOTAL PUNTOS POR PRUEBA = 100
FIN DE PRUEBA (END OF TEST)
REVISA TU TRABAJO POR FAVOR (PLEASE CHECK YOUR WORK)

PAPEL ADICIONAL/NO FALTA NADA DE ESTA PÁGINA

(EXTRA PAPER)/(NOTHING IS MISSING FROM THIS PAGE)

Grade 7
Term 3
PRACTICE TEST 2
CHILE
PABLO NERUDA
PARQUE NACIONAL TORRES DEL PAINE
DESIERTO DE ATACAMA

No cometas los mismos errores

(Don't make the same mistakes)

Below are common mistakes made by students of Spanish. Please note the mistakes and the corrections given. By avoiding these mistakes, you will be sure to improve your writing skills in Spanish.

PUNTUACIÓN Y MAYÚSCULAS (PUNCTUATION AND CAPITALIZATION)		
Inglés	Español con error	Español correcto
1. I don't like winter.	No me gusta el Invierno.	No me gusta el invierno.
2. What is your house like?	Cómo es tu casa?	¿Cómo es tu casa?
3. Your dress is beautiful!	Tu vestido es bonito!	¡Tu vestido es bonito!
4. Spring is in April.	La primavera es en Abril.	La primavera es en abril.
5. I like African clothes.	Me gusta la ropa Africana.	Me gusta la ropa africana.

LETRAS CON TILDES (LETTERS WITH TILDES)		
Inglés	Español con error	Español correcto
1. Do you like autumn?	¿Te gusta el otono?	¿Te gusta el otoño?
2. I have a big television.	Tengo una television grande.	Tengo una televisión grande.
3. Where are you?	¿Donde estás?	¿Dónde estás?
4. There are two bathrooms.	Hay dos cuartos de bano.	Hay dos cuartos de baño.
5. The belt is very long.	El cinturon es muy largo.	El cinturón es muy largo.

EL VOCABULARIO (VOCABULARY)		
Inglés	Español con error	Español correcto
1. He like the blouse.	A él le gusta la bolsa.	A él le gusta la blusa.
2. The shirt is large.	La camisa es larga.	La camisa es grande.
3. She has one hundred skirts.	Ella tiene ciento faldas.	Ella tiene cien faldas.
4. In the summer it very hot.	En el verano hace muy calor.	En el verano hace mucho calor.
5. The carpet is red.	La carpeta es roja.	La alfombra es roja.

Respuestas Abiertas (Free Response)

Nombre:_____________________________ Apellido: ________________________

Clase:_______________________________ Profesor/a: ______________________

Fecha: ____

Duración: 90 minutos

INSTRUCCIONES

1. **Esta prueba tiene CUATRO (4) secciones. Responde a cada pregunta en este papel.**

   This test has FOUR (4) sections. Answer all questions on this paper.

2. **Sección I: Tiene DIEZ (10) situaciones. Responde a cada situación en ESPAÑOL.**

   Section I: Has TEN (10) situations. Respond to each in SPANISH.

3. **Sección II: Tiene una carta informal. Escribe la carta en ESPAÑOL.**

   Section II: Has an informal letter. Write the letter in SPANISH.

4. **Sección III: Tiene un diálogo. Rellena los espacios en ESPAÑOL.**

   Section III: Has a dialogue. Complete the dialogue in SPANISH.

5. **Sección IV: Tiene una comprensión de lectura. Responde a las DIEZ (10) preguntas en INGLÉS.**

   Section IV: Has a reading comprehension. Answer the TEN (10) questions in ENGLISH.

Venezuela

SECCIÓN I

LAS SITUACIONES ESCRITAS (WRITTEN SITUATIONS)
RESPONDE A CADA SITUACIÓN (RESPOND TO EACH SITUATION)

1. **Write in SPANISH the information required by each of the situations given below. Do NOT write more than ONE sentence for each situation. For some situations, a complete sentence may not be necessary. Write each answer in the space provided.**

   (a) Your Chilean friend wants to know the date of a holiday in your country. What information do you email him/her?

   (3 puntos)

   ____

   (b) You want to know when your Mexican friend's birthday is. What do you ask him/her online?

   (3 puntos)

   ____

   (c) You are at your Chilean friend's house but he/she in not there and you cannot find something. Send him/her a text message asking where it is.

   (3 puntos)

   ____

   (d) You are going for dinner. On *Messenger*, your Venezuelan friend asks you what you are wearing. What do you reply?

   (3 puntos)

   ____

   (e) It is Spanish Day at your school. What do you write on the banner that you put at the front of the school?

   (3 puntos)

   ____

(f) You are creating a profile online in Spanish. What information do you write about yourself on your page?

(3 puntos)

____

(g) You are filling out an application form for a Spanish competition and one question asks you your family name (surname). What information do you write?

(3 puntos)

____

(h) You are doing your art project and get a text message in Spanish from a classmate asking which colours you are using. What do you reply?

(3 puntos)

____

(i) The Cuban embassy has asked students to write about their Spanish teachers on its website. What do you write?

(3 puntos)

____

(j) You want your Panamanian friend to describe something. What do you ask him/her in the email you send?

(3 puntos)

____

Sección I Total = 30 Puntos

CHILE

PABLO NERUDA

PARQUE NACIONAL TORRES DEL PAIN

DESIERTO DE ATACAMA

SECCIÓN II

LA CARTA INFORMAL (INFORMAL LETTER)
ESCRIBE UNA CARTA EN ESPAÑOL (WRITE A LETTER IN SPANISH)

2. **Using the following outline as a guide, write a letter in SPANISH of no more than 40 – 50 words.**

YOU WILL BE PENALIZED FOR DISREGARDING THESE INSTRUCTIONS.

The Colombian embassy has a competition entitled "My Ideal House" which requires that students write an informal letter to anyone about their ideal house. You enter the competition. Include:

(i) a description of your ideal house

(ii) some rooms in your ideal house

(iii) at least THREE (3) things that are in the house

(iv) the number of rooms in total in the house

____

____

____

____

____

____

____

____

____

____

____

____

____

____

(Do NOT write your real name and address, but include the date in Spanish and use the appropriate beginning and ending.)

Sección II Total = 30 Puntos

SECCIÓN III

EL DIÁLOGO CONTEXTUAL (CONTEXTUAL DIALOGUE)
LEE Y RELLENA EL DIÁLOGO EN ESPAÑOL
(READ AND COMPLETE THE DIALOGUE IN SPANISH)

CHILE

PABLO NERUDA

3. Use 40 – 50 words to complete the dialogue between you and an interviewer for Caribbean Magazine, giving your responses in SPANISH.

You were selected by your school to be interviewed by Caribbean Magazine. Complete the online conversation about the Caribbean by including:

(i) your Caribbean country

(ii) a description of Caribbean people

(iii) your favourite Caribbean country

(iv) any THREE (3) Caribbean countries

(v) a river in the Caribbean

Responses to ALL the cues provided must be included in the completed dialogue.

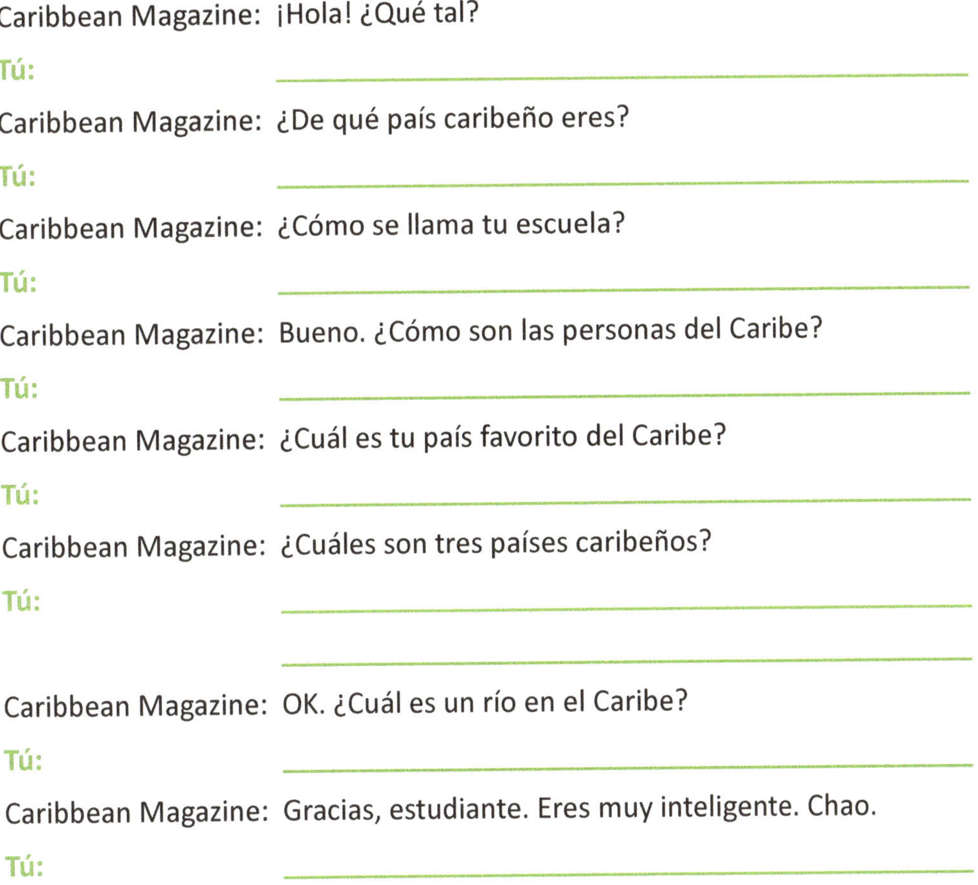

Caribbean Magazine: ¡Hola! ¿Qué tal?

Tú: ______________________________

Caribbean Magazine: ¿De qué país caribeño eres?

Tú: ______________________________

Caribbean Magazine: ¿Cómo se llama tu escuela?

Tú: ______________________________

Caribbean Magazine: Bueno. ¿Cómo son las personas del Caribe?

Tú: ______________________________

Caribbean Magazine: ¿Cuál es tu país favorito del Caribe?

Tú: ______________________________

Caribbean Magazine: ¿Cuáles son tres países caribeños?

Tú: ______________________________

____

Caribbean Magazine: OK. ¿Cuál es un río en el Caribe?

Tú: ______________________________

Caribbean Magazine: Gracias, estudiante. Eres muy inteligente. Chao.

Tú: ______________________________

PARQUE NACIONAL TORRES DEL PAINE

DESIERTO DE ATACAMA

Sección III Total = 20 Puntos

Bolivia

SECCIÓN IV

COMPRENSIÓN DE LECTURA (READING COMPREHENSION)
RESPONDE A CADA PREGUNTA (ANSWER ALL QUESTIONS)

4. Lee la siguiente selección con cuidado y responde a las preguntas en INGLÉS.

Read the following selection carefully. Do NOT translate but answer the questions in ENGLISH.

YOU WILL BE PENALIZED FOR DISREGARDING THESE INSTRUCTIONS.

Crop Over in Barbados

La isla caribeña de Barbados tiene muchos festivales pero el festival más popular y grande del país es el festival de 'Crop Over'. Cada verano en los meses de junio, julio y agosto, los barbadenses celebran el festival de 'Crop Over'. El festival comenzó* en los años 1780 y el festival es muy colorido. Por ejemplo, hay colores como anaranjado, amarillo, verde y más. El nombre 'Crop Over' representa el cultivo* de (caña de) azúcar*.

En el festival de 'Crop Over' hay la música calipso y arte bonito. Hay actividades para los niños y los adultos. A la cantante internacional barbadense, Robyn "Rihanna" Fenty le gusta el festival. El día final de 'Crop Over' se llama 'Kadooment' o 'Gran Kadooment'. Este festival es un evento especial para todos los barbadenses.

(130 palabras)

· La alpaca
· El Lago Titicaca

***comenzó – started/began**
***cultivo – crop/cultivation**
***caña de azúcar – sugar cane**

Answer the questions in ENGLISH, based on the selection above. Use a complete sentence for each response.

(a) Which words are used to describe the festival? **(2 puntos)**

____

(b) In which months does this festival take place? **(3 puntos)**

____

(c) When did this festival start? (1 punto)

____

(d) What are some colours at the festival? (3 puntos)

____

(e) Why is the festival called 'Crop Over'? (2 puntos)

____

(f) What can you hear and see at the festival? (2 puntos)

____

(g) For whom are there specially arranged activities? (2 puntos)

____

(h) What is said about Rihanna? (2 puntos)

____

(i) What is 'Kadooment'? (1 punto)

____

(j) What is said about the festival at the end? (2 puntos)

____

Sección IV Total = 20 Puntos

TOTAL PUNTOS POR PRUEBA = 100
FIN DE PRUEBA (END OF TEST)
REVISA TU TRABAJO POR FAVOR (PLEASE CHECK YOUR WORK)

CHILE

PABLO NERUDA

PARQUE NACIONAL TORRES DEL PAIN

DESIERTO DE ATACAMA

PAPEL ADICIONAL/NO FALTA NADA DE ESTA PÁGINA

(EXTRA PAPER)/(NOTHING IS MISSING FROM THIS PAGE)

(Eighth Grade)

Term 1 (Septiembre – Diciembre)

1. Revision
2. Aches/pains/illnesses
3. School
4. Possession
5. Restaurant (1)
6. Spare time activities
7. Chores
8. Shopping

Term 2 (Enero – Marzo/Abril)

1. More body parts
2. Community
3. Places to visit/ Places of interest
4. School extra-curricular activities
5. Transportation
6. Meals (breakfast, lunch, dinner)
7. Where are you going?
8. What are you going to do?

Term 3 (Abril/Mayo – Junio)

1. What do you do?
2. What are you doing?
3. What do you want to do?
4. What do you prefer?
5. What do you think?
6. Outside activities
7. What I enjoy/ like (to do) most.
8. Daily routine.

GRADE 8/ SECOND FORM

Funciones Comunicativas — Communicative Functions

Term 1	Term 2	Term 3
1. **Asking cost** - ¿Cuánto cuesta?/ ¿Cuánto es?	1. **Advising** – Hay que + verb/ Debes + verb	1. **Asking permission** - ¿Puedo + verb...?
2. **Enquiring about ill-ness** - ¿Qué te pasa?/ ¿Qué tienes?	2. **Describing commu-nity** – Es vieja/ moderna/ tranquila/ ruidosa/ pintoresca.	2. **Expressing inability to do something** – No puedo...
3. **Expressing ownership** – Es mío/ mía/ tuyo/ tuya/ suyo/ suya/ nuestro/ nuestra	3. **Expressing future plans** – Voy a + verb Voy a estudiar / Voy a jugar deportes	3. **Expressing thoughts/ opinions** – Yo pienso ...
4. **Expressing spare-time activities** – Yo nado/ Yo leo/ Yo bailo/ Yo escucho la música	4. **Expressing where you are going** – Voy a/al + place/ Voy al cine/ Voy al parque/ Voy a la escuela.	4. **Extending good wishes** – Buena suerte
5. **Identifying stores/ shops** – Es una panadería/ una frutería/ una carnicería/ una tienda	5. **Outlining study routine** –Estudio por dos horas cada día/ Estudio dos asignaturas cada noche.	5. **Sharing desires** – Quiero / Quisiera / Deseo
6. **Introducing others** – Te presento a ... / Éste es.../ Ésta es...	6. **Stating means of transportation** – (Yo) viajo por taxi/ Viajo por carro/ Viajo por autobús	6. **Stating current actions** – (Yo) estoy bailando/ Estoy estudiando/ Estoy leyendo etc.
7. **Providing information about your country** – Es un paraíso/ Es maravilloso/ Es bello.	7. **Stating preferences** – (Yo) prefiero	
8. **Stating favourite meals/ beverages** – Mi plato favorito es.../ Mi bebida favorita es...		
9. **Wishing a speedy recovery** - ¡Qué te mejores pronto!		

Grade 8

Term 1

PRACTICE TEST 1

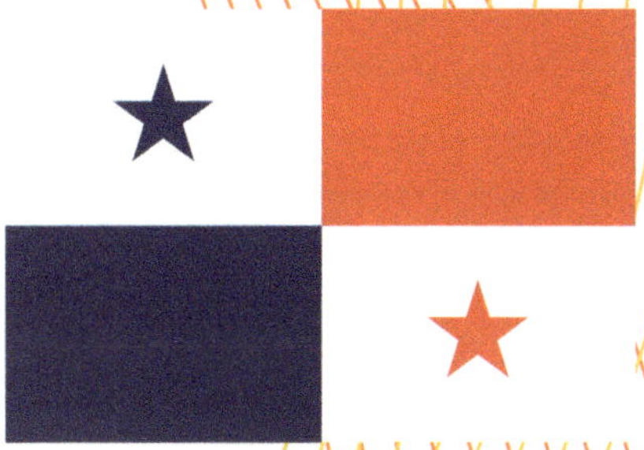

PANAMÁ

EL SOMBRERO DE PANAMÁ (PANAMÁ HAT)

LA ARPÍA MAYOR

EL CANAL DE PANAMÁ

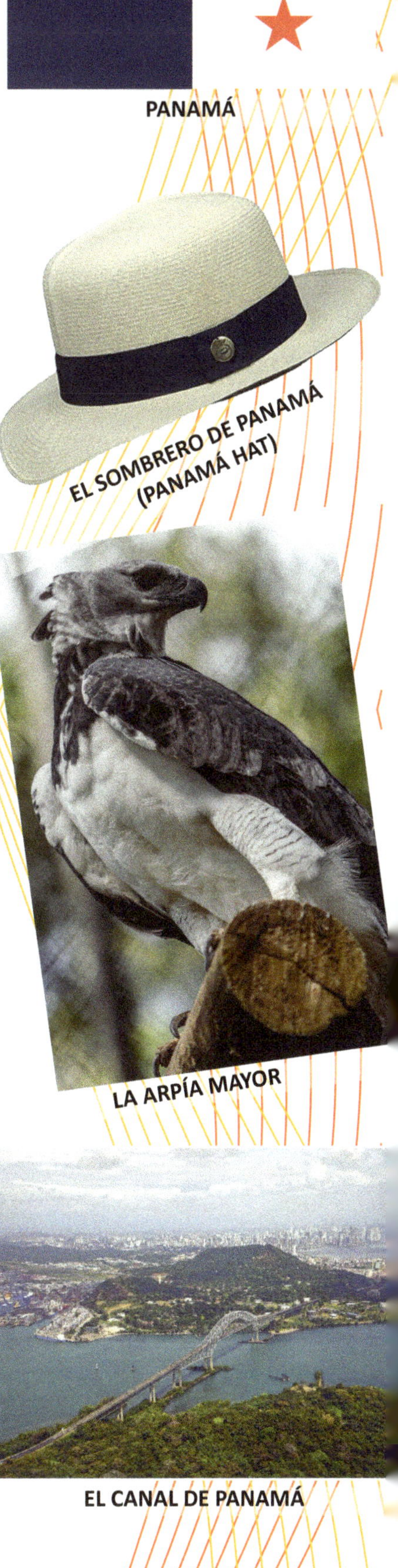

No cometas los mismos errores

(Don't make the same mistakes)

Below are common mistakes made by students of Spanish. Please note the mistakes and the corrections given. By avoiding these mistakes, you will be sure to improve your writing skills in Spanish.

LA GRAMÁTICA (GRAMMAR)		
Inglés	**Español con error**	**Español correcto**
1. October 12, 2024.	El 12 de octubre de 2020.	12 de octubre de 2020.
2. The watches are mine.	Los relojes son mío.	Los relojes son míos.
3. My mother and father like to cook.	A mi madre y mi padre gusta cocinar.	A mi madre y mi padre les gusta cocinar.
4. I like books very much.	Me gustan los libros muy mucho.	Me gustan los libros mucho.
5. I have a problem.	Tengo una problema.	Tengo un problema.

LA ORTOGRAFÍA (SPELLING)		
Inglés	**Español con error**	**Español correcto**
1. This restaurant has pizza.	Este restarante tiene pizza.	Este restaurante tiene pizza.
2. I want fried chicken.	Yo quiero poyo frito.	Yo quiero pollo frito.
3. The food is delicious.	La comida es deliciousa.	La comida es deliciosa.
4. My head hurts.	Me duele la cabesa.	Me duele la cabeza.
5. I wash my clothes.	Yo labo mi ropa.	Yo lavo mi ropa.

EL ORDEN DE LAS PALABRAS (WORD ORDER)		
Inglés	**Español con error**	**Español correcto**
1. My stomach hurts.	Mi estómago duele.	Me duele el estómago.
2. She has short hair.	Ella tiene corto pelo.	Ella tiene el pelo corto.
3. I like the French food.	Me gusta la francesa comida.	Me gusta la comida francesa.
4. My favorite hobby is watching TV.	Mi favorito pasatiempo es mirar la televisión.	Mi pasatiempo favorito es mirar la televisión.

Respuestas Abiertas (Free Response)

Nombre:__________________________ Apellido: ______________________

Clase:____________________________ Profesor/a: _____________________

Fecha: ____

Duración: 90 minutos

INSTRUCCIONES

1. **Esta prueba tiene CUATRO (4) secciones. Responde a cada pregunta en este papel.**

   This test has FOUR (4) sections. Answer all questions on this paper.

2. **Sección I: Tiene DIEZ (10) situaciones. Responde a cada situación en ESPAÑOL.**

   Section I: Has TEN (10) situations. Respond to each in SPANISH.

3. **Sección II: Tiene una carta informal. Escribe la carta en ESPAÑOL.**

   Section II: Has an informal letter. Write the letter in SPANISH.

4. **Sección III: Tiene un diálogo. Rellena los espacios en ESPAÑOL.**

   Section III: Has a dialogue. Complete the dialogue in SPANISH.

5. **Sección IV: Tiene una comprensión de lectura. Responde a las DIEZ (10) preguntas en INGLÉS.**

   Section IV: Has a reading comprehension. Answer the TEN (10) questions in ENGLISH.

Guatemala

SECCIÓN I

LAS SITUACIONES ESCRITAS (WRITTEN SITUATIONS)
RESPONDE A CADA SITUACIÓN (RESPOND TO EACH SITUATION)

1. **Write in SPANISH the information required by each of the situations given below. Do NOT write more than ONE sentence for each situation. For some situations, a complete sentence may not be necessary. Write each answer in the space provided.**

(a) You are having a party for your Costa Rican friend who is visiting you. What do you write on the banner you make?

(3 puntos)

____

(b) You have formed a *WhatsApp* group with two of your friends who speak Spanish. How do you introduce them to each other?

(3 puntos)

____

(c) Your Panamanian friend has sent you a picture of a Panamanian hat that he/she has bought for you. What message do you send him/her?

(3 puntos)

____

(d) You want to know your Uruguayan friend's favourite relative. What do you ask him/her in the message you send?

(3 puntos)

____

(e) Your Colombian friend sends you a message asking if you like black chocolate or white chocolate. What do you reply?

(3 puntos)

____

(f) The Spanish Association in your country has asked you to write about your school . What do you write?

(3 puntos)

___

(g) Your Bolivian friend has said that he/she has a lot of cousins and asks how many cousins you have. How do you reply on *Instagram*?

(3 puntos)

___

(h) Your Nicaraguan pen pal sent you a text message asking you the cost of an apple in your country. What do you reply?

(3 puntos)

___

(i) A Guatemalan student is coming to visit your country and sends you a message asking you to name a beautiful place in your country. What do you reply?

(3 puntos)

___

(j) Your Cuban friend emails you and asks if you like clothes. What do you reply?

(3 puntos)

___

PANAMÁ
EL SOMBRERO DE PANAMÁ (PANAMÁ HAT)
LA ARPÍA MAYOR
EL CANAL DE PANAMÁ

Sección I Total = 30 Puntos

SECCIÓN II

LA CARTA INFORMAL (INFORMAL LETTER)
ESCRIBE UNA CARTA EN ESPAÑOL (WRITE A LETTER IN SPANISH)

2. **Using the following outline as a guide, write a letter in SPANISH of no more than 50 – 60 words.**

YOU WILL BE PENALIZED FOR DISREGARDING THESE INSTRUCTIONS.

You and your friends are planning to go shopping one day. Write a letter to your Uruguayan friend in which you include:

(i) when and where you are going shopping

(ii) some of the things you are going to buy

(iii) some types of stores/shops in your country

(iv) what you like to buy

____

____

____

____

____

____

____

____

____

____

____

____

____

____

(Do NOT write your real name and address, but include the date in Spanish and use the appropriate beginning and ending.)

Sección II Total = 30 Puntos

SECCIÓN III

EL DIÁLOGO CONTEXTUAL (CONTEXTUAL DIALOGUE)
LEE Y RELLENA EL DIÁLOGO EN ESPAÑOL
(READ AND COMPLETE THE DIALOGUE IN SPANISH)

3. **Use 50 – 60 words to complete the dialogue between you and your Costa Rican friend, giving your responses in SPANISH.**

   You are sick at home and your Costa Rican friend sends you some messages on *Instagram*. Complete the dialogue you have with him/her. Be sure to include:

   (i) greeting and how you're doing
   (ii) what sickness you have
   (iii) when you are going to the doctor
   (iv) what you are doing to get better
   (v) who helps to take care of you at home

Responses to ALL the cues provided must be included in the completed dialogue.

Amigo/a: ¡Epa! ¿Qué tal?

Tú: ______________________________

Amigo/a: ¡Dios mío! ¿Qué te pasa?

Tú: ______________________________

Amigo/a: ¡Caramba! ¿Tienes dolor del estómago y la garganta también?

Tú: ______________________________

Amigo/a: ¿Cuándo vas al médico?

Tú: ______________________________

Amigo/a: ¿Tienes frutas en casa? La vitamina es muy importante.

Tú: ______________________________

Amigo/a: ¿Bebes mucha agua y jugo?

Tú: ______________________________

Amigo/a: ¿Descansas mucho?

Tú: ______________________________

Amigo/a: ¿Cuántas horas al día descansas?

Tú: ______________________________

Amigo/a: Bueno. ¡Qué te mejores pronto! Hasta luego.

Tú: ______________________________

Sección III Total =20 Puntos

PANAMÁ

EL SOMBRERO DE PANAMÁ (PANAMÁ HAT)

LA ARPÍA MAYOR

EL CANAL DE PANAMÁ

Trinidad y Tobago

SECCIÓN IV

COMPRENSIÓN DE LECTURA (READING COMPREHENSION)
RESPONDE A CADA PREGUNTA (ANSWER ALL QUESTIONS)

4. **Lee la siguiente selección con cuidado y responde a las preguntas en INGLÉS.**

Read the following selection carefully. Do NOT translate but answer the questions in ENGLISH.

YOU WILL BE PENALIZED FOR DISREGARDING THESE INSTRUCTIONS.

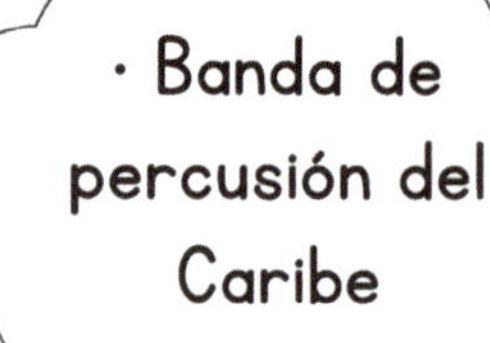

Trinidad and Tobago Carnival

El carnaval de Trinidad y Tobago es un evento muy grande en la isla cada año. Normalmente, el evento es el lunes y el martes antes* del Miércoles de la Ceniza* en el mes de febrero o marzo. Las personas al carnaval escuchan y bailan a la música calipso y especialmente soca. También, tocan la música en el instrumento nacional de Trinidad y Tobago, el *steel pan*. Ellos caminan en la calle en ropa colorida, bonita y brillante.

Cada febrero o marzo, miles de personas viajan a Trinidad por el carnaval. A las cuatro de la mañana el día del carnaval (el lunes), muchas personas participan en 'J'Ouvert'. 'J'Ouvert' es una fiesta grande en la calle. El carnaval es un evento cultural en el país y la comida y el ron son muy importantes al carnaval.

(136 palabras)

***antes de-before**
***ceniza-Ash**

Answer the questions in ENGLISH, based on the selection above. Use a complete sentence for each response.

(a) How often is carnival held in Trinidad and Tobago? (1 punto)

____

(b) On which days does the carnival take place? (2 puntos)

____

(c) What is said about February and March? (2 puntos)

____

(d) What do people do at the carnival? (2 puntos)

____

(e) What is said about the *steel pan*? (2 puntos)

____

(f) What THREE (3) types of music are mentioned? (3 puntos)

____

(g) Describe the carnival costumes. (3 puntos)

____

(h) How many people go to the carnival? (1 punto)

____

(i) When is 'J'Ouvert'? (2 puntos)

____

(j) Which TWO (2) things are said to be important to the carnival? (2 puntos)

____

EL CANAL DE PANAMÁ

Sección IV Total = 20 Puntos

TOTAL PUNTOS POR PRUEBA = 100
FIN DE PRUEBA (END OF TEST)
REVISA TU TRABAJO POR FAVOR (PLEASE CHECK YOUR WORK)

PAPEL ADICIONAL/NO FALTA NADA DE ESTA PÁGINA

(EXTRA PAPER)/(NOTHING IS MISSING FROM THIS PAGE)

Grade 8

Term 1

PRACTICE TEST 2

LA REPÚBLICA DOMINICANA

SANCOCHO

MUÑECAS LIMÉ

MERENGUE

No cometas los mismos errores

(Don't make the same mistakes)

Below are common mistakes made by students of Spanish. Please note the mistakes and the corrections given. By avoiding these mistakes, you will be sure to improve your writing skills in Spanish.

PUNTUACIÓN Y MAYÚSCULAS (PUNCTUATION AND CAPITALIZATION)		
Inglés	**Español con error**	**Español correcto**
1. My favourite book is 'Yellow Rain'.	Mi libro favorito es 'La Lluvia Amarilla'	Mi libro favorito es 'La lluvia amarilla'.
2. It is Spanish bread.	Es el pan Español.	Es el pan español.
3. I wash the dishes on Mondays.	Yo lavo los platos los Lunes.	Yo lavo los platos los lunes.
4. Who irons your uniform?	Quién plancha tu uniforme?	¿Quién plancha tu uniforme?
5. The bill, please!	La cuenta, por favor!	¡La cuenta, por favor!

LETRAS CON TILDES (LETTERS WITH TILDES)		
Inglés	**Español con error**	**Español correcto**
1. The pen is mine.	La pluma es mia.	La pluma es mía.
2. My wrist hurts.	Me duele la muneca.	Me duele la muñeca.
3. Is there a menu?	¿Hay un menu?	¿Hay un menú?
4. My school is not small.	Mi escuela no es pequena.	Mi escuela no es pequeña.
5. We play football.	Nosotros jugamos al futbol.	Nosotros jugamos al fútbol.

EL VOCABULARIO (VOCABULARY)		
Inglés	**Español con error**	**Español correcto**
1. I play the piano.	Yo juego el piano.	Yo toco el piano.
2. He has long legs.	Él tiene pies largos.	Él tiene piernas largas.
3. Everyday I play games.	Cada día yo juego jugos.	Cada día yo juego juegos.
4. The fish is delicious.	El pez es delicioso.	El pescado es delicioso.
5. I want tea.	Yo quiero te.	Yo quiero té.

Respuestas Abiertas (Free Response)

Nombre:_________________________ Apellido: _____________________

Clase:_________________________ Profesor/a: _____________________

Fecha: ____

Duración: 90 minutos

INSTRUCCIONES

1. **Esta prueba tiene CUATRO (4) secciones. Responde a cada pregunta en este papel.**

   This test has FOUR (4) sections. Answer all questions on this paper.

2. **Sección I: Tiene DIEZ (10) situaciones. Responde a cada situación en ESPAÑOL.**

   Section I: Has TEN (10) situations. Respond to each in SPANISH.

3. **Sección II: Tiene una carta informal. Escribe la carta en ESPAÑOL.**

   Section II: Has an informal letter. Write the letter in SPANISH.

4. **Sección III: Tiene un diálogo. Rellena los espacios en ESPAÑOL.**

   Section III: Has a dialogue. Complete the dialogue in SPANISH.

5. **Sección IV: Tiene una comprensión de lectura. Responde a las DIEZ (10) preguntas en INGLÉS.**

   Section IV: Has a reading comprehension. Answer the TEN (10) questions in ENGLISH.

Uruguay

SECCIÓN I

LAS SITUACIONES ESCRITAS (WRITTEN SITUATIONS)
RESPONDE A CADA SITUACIÓN (RESPOND TO EACH SITUATION)

1. Write in SPANISH the information required by each of the situations given below. Do NOT write more than ONE sentence for each situation. For some situations, a complete sentence may not be necessary. Write each answer in the space provided.

(a) The new student in your class who is from the Dominican Republic sends you a note asking you what kind of clothes you like. What do you write in the note?

(3 puntos)

___

(b) You want your Venezuelan friend to describe one of his/her relatives. What do you ask in the text message that you send him/her?

(3 puntos)

___

(c) Someone lost an item and a classmate sends a picture of the item in the Spanish *WhatsApp* group asking to whom it belongs. What do you reply?

(3 puntos)

___

(d) Your Mexican friend wants to know what they eat in your country. Reply to his message by listing two things.

(3 puntos)

___

(e) Your school is closed today because of heavy rains. Send an email to your friend from Spain telling him/how you feel today.

(3 puntos)

___

(f) Your Peruvian friend wants to know what you do for fun. What do you reply in the email you send him/her?

(3 puntos)

____

LA REPÚBLICA DOMINICANA

(g) Your Costa Rican friend asks how many subjects you have on Mondays. What do you reply?

(3 puntos)

____

SANCOCHO

(h) A new Argentine student at your school wants to know where a particular place in the school is. What does he/she ask in the note he/she sends you?

(3 puntos)

____

(i) You are thirsty, so your classmate goes to the cafeteria and sends you a message in Spanish asking what do you like to drink. What do you reply?

(3 puntos)

____

MUÑECAS LIMÉ

(j) You went to buy something but were surprised at the price. What do you tell your Colombian friend about the price in the message you send him/her?

(3 puntos)

____

Sección I Total = 30 Puntos

MERENGUE

LA CARTA INFORMAL (INFORMAL LETTER)
ESCRIBE UNA CARTA EN ESPAÑOL (WRITE A LETTER IN SPANISH)

2. **Using the following outline as a guide, write a letter in SPANISH of no more than 50 – 60 words.**

YOU WILL BE PENALIZED FOR DISREGARDING THESE INSTRUCTIONS.

You have met a new Argentinian friend who has written you about some of his/her activities. Write him/her a letter about yourself and include:

(i) at least THREE (3) activities you do in your spare time
(ii) some of your household chores
(iii) what any two of your family members do at home
(iv) where you like to go with your friends

____

____

____

____

____

____

____

____

____

____

____

____

____

____

(Do NOT write your real name and address, but include the date in Spanish and use the appropriate beginning and ending.)

Sección II Total = 30 Puntos

SECCIÓN III

EL DIÁLOGO CONTEXTUAL (CONTEXTUAL DIALOGUE)
LEE Y RELLENA EL DIÁLOGO EN ESPAÑOL
(READ AND COMPLETE THE DIALOGUE IN SPANISH)

LA REPÚBLICA DOMINICANA

3. **Use 50 – 60 words to complete the dialogue between you and your friend from Equatorial Guinea, giving your responses in SPANISH.**

You are having a *WhatsApp* conversation with your Spanish-speaking friend from Africa who wants to know about you and your friends. Complete the conversation and include:

(i) how many friends you have
(ii) where you and your friends go together
(iii) what you and your friends do
(iv) whether you visit your friends' house or not
(v) with which friend you like to go shopping

SANCOCHO

Responses to ALL the cues provided must be included in the completed dialogue.

Amigo/a: Hola. ¿Cuántos amigos tienes?

Tú: ______________________________

Amigo/a: ¿Cómo son?

Tú: ______________________________

Amigo/a: ¿Tienes muchos amigos en tu escuela?

Tú: ______________________________

Amigo/a: ¿Adónde vas con tus amigos normalmente?

Tú: ______________________________

MUÑECAS LIMÉ

Amigo/a: ¡Qué bueno! ¿Qué haces con tus amigos?

Tú: ______________________________

Amigo/a: ¡Interesante! ¿Cuándo van ustedes al cine o al centro comercial?

Tú: ______________________________

Amigo/a: ¿Visitas la casa de tus amigos?

Tú: ______________________________

Amigo/a: ¿Con qué amigo te gusta comprar los zapatos?

Tú: ______________________________

Amigo/a: Pues, eres mi buen/a amigo/a. Hasta luego.

Tú: ______________________________

MERENGUE

Sección III Total = 20 Puntos

Guyana

SECCIÓN IV

COMPRENSIÓN DE LECTURA (READING COMPREHENSION)
RESPONDE A CADA PREGUNTA (ANSWER ALL QUESTIONS)

4. Lee la siguiente selección con cuidado y responde a las preguntas en INGLÉS.

Read the following selection carefully. Do NOT translate but answer the questions in ENGLISH.

YOU WILL BE PENALIZED FOR DISREGARDING THESE INSTRUCTIONS.

<u>Guyana's Love of Cricket</u>

El críquet es un deporte de bate y pelota y es muy popular alrededor de las Antillas. En Guyana, no es diferente. Muchos jóvenes y adultos juegan el deporte en su tiempo libre. Pero, Guyana tiene muchos jugadores* profesionales del críquet. Estos jugadores son miembros del equipo* de críquet de Las Antillas. Unos de los jugadores más famosos del críquet guyanés son Clive Lloyd, Chivnarine Chanderpaul y Lance Gibbs.

Los jugadores del críquet guyanés representan su país y las Antillas muy bien. El 'Guyana Amazon Warriors' es un equipo que representa el país en un torneo* del críquet en el Caribe cada año. Normalmente el equipo es excelente. A más y más chicas y mujeres guyanesas les gusta jugar al críquet porque es muy popular y es un deporte por cada persona, no solo hombres o chicos.

(136 palabras)

***los jugadores-players**
***el equipo-team**
***el torneo-tournament**

Answer the questions in ENGLISH, based on the selection above. Use a complete sentence for each response.

(a) How is cricket described? **(2 puntos)**

____

(b) When do many Guyanese youngsters play cricket? **(2 puntos)**

____

(c) What is said about professional cricketers? (2 puntos)

___

(d) Which regional team do the cricketers form? (1 punto)

___

(e) List THREE (3) famous Guyanese cricketers. (3 puntos)

___

(f) How do Guyanese cricketers represent their country? (2 puntos)

___

(g) What is the 'Guyana Amazon Warriors'? (2 puntos)

___

(h) Which word is used to describe the team? (1 punto)

___

(i) Who are said to like to play cricket? (2 puntos)

___

(j) What is said about cricket and men? (3 puntos)

___

Sección IV Total = 20 Puntos

TOTAL PUNTOS POR PRUEBA = 100
FIN DE PRUEBA (END OF TEST)
REVISA TU TRABAJO POR FAVOR (PLEASE CHECK YOUR WORK)

LA REPÚBLICA DOMINICANA

SANCOCHO

MUÑECAS LIMÉ

MERENGUE

PAPEL ADICIONAL/NO FALTA NADA DE ESTA PÁGINA

(EXTRA PAPER)/(NOTHING IS MISSING FROM THIS PAGE)

BOLIVIA
(NAMED AFTER SIMÓN BOLÍVAR)

SOPA DE MANÍ

TIWANAKU

SALAR DE UYUNI

No cometas los mismos errores

(Don't make the same mistakes)

Below are common mistakes made by students of Spanish. Please note the mistakes and the corrections given. By avoiding these mistakes, you will be sure to improve your writing skills in Spanish.

LA GRAMÁTICA (GRAMMAR)		
Inglés	**Español con error**	**Español correcto**
1. I am going to school.	Soy voy a la escuela.	Voy a la escuela.
2. I travel by taxi.	Mi viajo por taxi.	Yo viajo por taxi.
3. She is going to the cinema.	Ella va a el cine.	Ella va al cine.
4. We eat dinner at 6 p.m.	Nosotros comer la cena a las seis de la tarde.	Nosotros comemos la cena a las seis de la tarde.
5. I am going to study.	Voy estudiar.	Voy a estudiar.

LA ORTOGRAFÍA (SPELLING)		
Inglés	**Español con error**	**Español correcto**
1. My community is big.	Mi communidad es grande.	Mi comunidad es grande.
2. For lunch, I want ham.	Por almuerso, quiero jamón.	Por almuerzo, quiero jamón.
3. I'm a member of the art club.	Soy miembro del clubo de arte.	Soy miembro del club de arte.
4. I play tennis.	Yo juego al tennis.	Yo juego al tenis.
5. My community has a bank.	Mi comunidad tiene un banko.	Mi comunidad tiene un banco.

EL ORDEN DE LAS PALABRAS (WORD ORDER)		
Inglés	**Español con error**	**Español correcto**
1. The drama club is fun.	El drama club es divertido.	El club de drama es divertido.
2. The human body has two eyes.	El humano cuerpo tiene dos ojos.	El cuerpo humano tiene dos ojos.
3. I live in a small community.	Vivo en una pequeña comunidad.	Vivo en una comunidad pequeña.
4. My back hurts.	La espalda me duele.	Me duele la espalda.

Respuestas Abiertas (Free Response)

Nombre:____________________________ Apellido: ________________________

Clase:______________________________ Profesor/a: ______________________

Fecha: ____

Duración: 90 minutos

INSTRUCCIONES

1. **Esta prueba tiene CUATRO (4) secciones. Responde a cada pregunta en este papel.**

   This test has FOUR (4) sections. Answer all questions on this paper.

2. **Sección I: Tiene DIEZ (10) situaciones. Responde a cada situación en ESPAÑOL.**

   Section I: Has TEN (10) situations. Respond to each in SPANISH.

3. **Sección II: Tiene una carta informal. Escribe la carta en ESPAÑOL.**

   Section II: Has an informal letter. Write the letter in SPANISH.

4. **Sección III: Tiene un diálogo. Rellena los espacios en ESPAÑOL.**

   Section III: Has a dialogue. Complete the dialogue in SPANISH.

5. **Sección IV: Tiene una comprensión de lectura. Responde a las DIEZ (10) preguntas en INGLÉS.**

   Section IV: Has a reading comprehension. Answer the TEN (10) questions in ENGLISH.

Belice

SECCIÓN I

LAS SITUACIONES ESCRITAS (WRITTEN SITUATIONS)
RESPONDE A CADA SITUACIÓN (RESPOND TO EACH SITUATION)

1. **Write in SPANISH the information required by each of the situations given below. Do NOT write more than ONE sentence for each situation. For some situations, a complete sentence may not be necessary. Write each answer in the space provided.**

(a) Your Peruvian classmate did not come to school today because he/she is sick. What do you ask him/her in the message that you send him/her?

(3 puntos)

____

(b) Your Venezuelan friend wants to know how many hours a day you study. What do you reply in your message on *Instagram*?

(3 puntos)

____

(c) Your Bolivian friend is coming to visit you on your island and asks if there is a park where you live. What do you reply?

(3 puntos)

____

(d) You receive a message from your Spanish-speaking friend on *Messenger* asking you who cooks in your house. What do you reply?

(3 puntos)

____

(e) Your school is conducting a survey in Spanish. One question asks what activity you do for the school. What do you write on the form?

(3 puntos)

____

(f) At a Spanish club meeting you are asked to write one sentence about where you live/your community. What do you write?

(3 puntos)

____

BOLIVIA
(NAMED AFTER SIMÓN BOLÍVAR)

(g) You receive an email Spanish from your friend who asks where you eat at school. What do you reply?

(3 puntos)

____

SOPA DE MANÍ

(h) You enter a Spanish competition to win concert tickets and a question asks you to type a sentence stating who your favourite singer is. What do you type?

(3 puntos)

____

(i) You will be celebrating your birthday soon so your friend from El Salvador sends you a message on *Facebook* asking where you are going. What do you reply?

(3 puntos)

____

TIWANAKU

(j) Your Uruguayan friend wants to know how you go to school. What do you text him/her?

(3 puntos)

____

SALAR DE UYUNI

Sección I Total = 30 Puntos

SECCIÓN II

LA CARTA INFORMAL (INFORMAL LETTER)
ESCRIBE UNA CARTA EN ESPAÑOL (WRITE A LETTER IN SPANISH)

2. Using the following outline as a guide, write a letter in SPANISH of no more than 50 – 60 words.

YOU WILL BE PENALIZED FOR DISREGARDING THESE INSTRUCTIONS.

You recently met a new friend from Nicaragua and he/she wants to know more about your eating habits. Write a letter to him/her in which you include:

(i) what you normally eat for breakfast

(ii) what kinds of vegetables you like

(iii) what time you usually eat lunch or dinner and what you eat

(iv) your favourite restaurant

(Do NOT write your real name and address, but include the date in Spanish and use the appropriate beginning and ending.)

Sección II Total = 30 Puntos

SECCIÓN III

EL DIÁLOGO CONTEXTUAL (CONTEXTUAL DIALOGUE)
LEE Y RELLENA EL DIÁLOGO EN ESPAÑOL
(READ AND COMPLETE THE DIALOGUE IN SPANISH)

BOLIVIA
(NAMED AFTER SIMÓN BOLÍVAR)

3. Use 50 – 60 words to complete the dialogue between you and your Guatemalan friend, giving your responses in SPANISH.

Your Guatemalan friend messages you online to find out about some of your activities outside of school. Complete the conversation between both of you by including:

(i) TV programmes you watch
(ii) how often you watch TV
(iii) when you listen to the radio
(iv) what you like to read
(v) whether you play videogames or not

Responses to ALL the cues provided must be included in the completed dialogue.

SOPA DE MANÍ

Amigo/a: ¡Epa! ¿Qué miras en la televisión?

Tú: ______________________________

Amigo/a: ¿Cuántas horas al día miras la televisión?

Tú: ______________________________

Amigo/a: ¿Miras la televisión solo/a o con tu familia?

Tú: ______________________________

TIWANAKU

Amigo/a: ¿Escuchas la radio cada día?

Tú: ______________________________

Amigo/a: ¿Qué escuchas en la radio normalmente?

Tú: ______________________________

Amigo/a: ¡Qué chévere! ¿Te gusta leer?

Tú: ______________________________

Amigo/a: ¿Qué te gusta leer?

Tú: ______________________________

SALAR DE UYUNI

Amigo/a: ¿Juegas los videojuegos?

Tú: ______________________________

Amigo/a: ¡Yo también! Nos vemos pronto. Chao.

Tú: ______________________________

Sección III Total = 20 Puntos

Las Islas Caimán

SECCIÓN IV

COMPRENSIÓN DE LECTURA (READING COMPREHENSION)
RESPONDE A CADA PREGUNTA (ANSWER ALL QUESTIONS)

4. **Lee la siguiente selección con cuidado y responde a las preguntas en INGLÉS.**

Read the following selection carefully. Do NOT translate but answer the questions in ENGLISH.

YOU WILL BE PENALIZED FOR DISREGARDING THESE INSTRUCTIONS.

Cayman Islands: Beautiful Waters, and Pirates.

Las Islas Caimán están situadas al sur de Cuba y al oeste de Jamaica. La Gran Caimán tiene dos 'hermanas islas'. Se llaman, 'La Caimán Brac' y 'El Pequeño Caimán'. La palabra 'Caimán' significa un reptil, un aligátor pequeño. Pero, las aguas del país caribeño son hermosas y ricas. Las aguas verdes y azules son limpias y puras. Hay muchas especies de animales acuáticos como peces y tortugas.

Las actividades acuáticas son populares en Caimán, por ejemplo, el surf, la pesca y nadar con los delfínes*. Cada año en el mes de noviembre, las tres islas del país tienen un festival de los piratas. El festival es una celebración de la cultura y la historia del país. También, hay mucha música y comida en el festival. Normalmente, hay muchos eventos en la semana de piratas.

(136 palabras)

***delfínes – dolphins**

Answer the questions in ENGLISH, based on the selection above. Use a complete sentence for each response.

(a) Where are the Cayman Islands located in relation to Cuba and Jamaica? **(2 puntos)**

____

(b) How many 'sister islands' does the Grand Cayman have? **(1 punto)**

____

(c) Which are the 'sister islands' of the Grand Cayman? (2 puntos)

____

(d) What does 'Cayman' mean? (2 puntos)

____

(e) Identify THREE (3) ways in which the islands' waters are described. (3 puntos)

____

(f) Which aquatic animals are mentioned? (2 puntos)

____

(g) Identify THREE (3) aquatic activities stated. (3 puntos)

____

(h) When is the pirates' festival held? (1 puntos)

____

(i) What does the festival celebrate? (2 puntos)

____

(j) What can be found at the festival? (2 puntos)

____

Sección IV Total = 20 Puntos

TOTAL PUNTOS POR PRUEBA = 100
FIN DE PRUEBA (END OF TEST)
REVISA TU TRABAJO POR FAVOR (PLEASE CHECK YOUR WORK)

BOLIVIA
(NAMED AFTER SIMÓN BOLÍVAR)

SOPA DE MANÍ

TIWANAKU

SALAR DE UYUNI

PAPEL ADICIONAL/NO FALTA NADA DE ESTA PÁGINA

(EXTRA PAPER)/(NOTHING IS MISSING FROM THIS PAGE)

PUERTO RICO
(RICH PORT)

PIÑA COLADA

MOFONGO

VIEJO SAN JUAN

No cometas los mismos errores

(Don't make the same mistakes)

Below are common mistakes made by students of Spanish. Please note the mistakes and the corrections given. By avoiding these mistakes, you will be sure to improve your writing skills in Spanish.

PUNTUACIÓN Y MAYÚSCULAS (PUNCTUATION AND CAPITALIZATION)		
Inglés	**Español con error**	**Español correcto**
1. What are you going to do?	Qué vas a hacer?	¿Qué vas a hacer?
2. On Saturday, I'm going to swim at the beach.	El Sábado, voy a nadar a la playa.	El sábado, voy a nadar a la playa.
3. Some Cubans are in my community.	Algunos Cubanos están en mi comunidad.	Algunos cubanos están en mi comunidad.
4. I'm going to the stadium!	Voy al estadio!	¡Voy al estadio!
5. Where are you going in March?	¿Adónde vas en Marzo?	¿Adónde vas en marzo?

LETRAS CON TILDES (LETTERS WITH TILDES)		
Inglés	**Español con error**	**Español correcto**
1. We travel by bus.	Nosotros viajamos por autobus.	Nosotros viajamos por autobús.
2. I'm going to the river.	Voy al rio.	Voy al río.
3. The Blue Mountain is a place of interest.	Las Montanas Azules es un lugar de interés.	Las Montañas Azules es un lugar de interés.
4. He travels by taxi.	El viaja por taxi.	Él viaja por taxi.
5. She's going to teach the class.	Ella va a ensenar la clase.	Ella va a enseñar la clase.

EL VOCABULARIO (VOCABULARY)		
Inglés	**Español con error**	**Español correcto**
1. She has one hundred and twenty books.	Ella tiene siento veinte libros.	Ella tiene ciento veinte libros.
2. When are you going?	¿Cuánto vas?	¿Cuándo vas?
3. I'm going to the library.	Yo voy a la librería.	Yo voy a la biblioteca.
4. Where are you going?	¿Dónde vas?	¿Adónde vas?
5. He is going to the park.	Él va al porque.	Él va al parque.

Respuestas Abiertas (Free Response)

Nombre:_________________________ Apellido: ____________________

Clase:___________________________ Profesor/a: ___________________

Fecha: ____

Duración: 90 minutos

INSTRUCCIONES

1. **Esta prueba tiene CUATRO (4) secciones. Responde a cada pregunta en este papel.**

   This test has FOUR (4) sections. Answer all questions on this paper.

2. **Sección I: Tiene DIEZ (10) situaciones. Responde a cada situación en ESPAÑOL.**

   Section I: Has TEN (10) situations. Respond to each in SPANISH.

3. **Sección II: Tiene una carta informal. Escribe la carta en ESPAÑOL.**

   Section II: Has an informal letter. Write the letter in SPANISH.

4. **Sección III: Tiene un diálogo. Rellena los espacios en ESPAÑOL.**

   Section III: Has a dialogue. Complete the dialogue in SPANISH.

5. **Sección IV: Tiene una comprensión de lectura. Responde a las DIEZ (10) preguntas en INGLÉS.**

   Section IV: Has a reading comprehension. Answer the TEN (10) questions in ENGLISH.

SECCIÓN I

LAS SITUACIONES ESCRITAS (WRITTEN SITUATIONS)
RESPONDE A CADA SITUACIÓN (RESPOND TO EACH SITUATION)

Me gusta ir al cine.

1. **Write in SPANISH the information required by each of the situations given below. Do NOT write more than ONE sentence for each situation. For some situations, a complete sentence may not be necessary. Write each answer in the space provided.**

   (a) You recently received a message on *WhatsApp* in Spanish asking you if you sing well. What do you reply in the sentence you send?

   (3 puntos)

   ____

   (b) Your Spanish teacher has asked each student to write a sentence stating which of their facial features they like. What do you write?

   (3 puntos)

   ____

   (c) A Panamanian student is visiting your school for a month. He/she sends you a note asking if you have a dictionary. What do you write in the note?

   (3 puntos)

   ____

   (d) Your Mexican friend has made a post on *Facebook* asking people what they do on Saturdays. Reply to his/her post.

   (3 puntos)

   ____

   (e) Your friend from Spain has asked you one reason he/she should visit the Caribbean. What do you reply in the email you send?

   (3 puntos)

   ____

(f) One of your Puerto Rican friends sends you a message on *Snapchat* asking you what he/she needs to do to get good grades in school. What do you reply?

(3 puntos)

____

PUERTO RICO (RICH PORT)

PIÑA COLADA

(g) You receive a questionnaire in Spanish asking about your community and in particular, about one facility that your community needs. What do you write?

(3 puntos)

____

(h) You want to know when your friend from Peru does a particular activity. What do you ask him/her in the email you send him/her?

(3 puntos)

____

(i) Tomorrow is 'Business Day' at school. Send your Spanish teacher a message telling him/her what you are going to sell.

(3 puntos)

____

MOFONGO

(j) Your Cuban friend sends you a text message asking if there are taxis in your country. What do you reply in the message you send him/her?

(3 puntos)

____

VIEJO SAN JUAN

Sección I Total = 30 Puntos

LA CARTA INFORMAL (INFORMAL LETTER)
ESCRIBE UNA CARTA EN ESPAÑOL (WRITE A LETTER IN SPANISH)

2. Using the following outline as a guide, write a letter in SPANISH of no more than 50 – 60 words.

YOU WILL BE PENALIZED FOR DISREGARDING THESE INSTRUCTIONS.

You are going to have your birthday soon. Write a letter to your Bolivian friend telling him/her about your plans. Be sure to:

(i) say when your birthday is
(i) state what you are going to do for your birthday
(i) include TWO (2) things you need for your birthday
(i) mention where you and your friends are going

____

____

____

____

____

____

____

____

____

____

____

____

____

____

(Do NOT write your real name and address, but include the date in Spanish and use the appropriate beginning and ending.)

Sección II Total = 30 Puntos

SECCIÓN III

EL DIÁLOGO CONTEXTUAL (CONTEXTUAL DIALOGUE)
LEE Y RELLENA EL DIÁLOGO EN ESPAÑOL
(READ AND COMPLETE THE DIALOGUE IN SPANISH)

PUERTO RICO (RICH PORT)

PIÑA COLADA

MOFONGO

3. Use 50 – 60 words to complete the dialogue between you and your Argentinian friend, giving your responses in SPANISH.

Your Argentinian friend starts a conversation with you online about studying. Complete the conversation by including:

(i) your wellbeing and location
(ii) what you are doing
(iii) which subject you dislike studying
(iv) whether you use the internet to study or not
(v) whether you study with friends or not

Responses to ALL the cues provided must be included in the completed dialogue.

Amigo/a: ¡Eh! ¿Qué tal y dónde estás?

Tú: ______________________________

Amigo/a: ¿Qué estás haciendo tú?

Tú: ______________________________

Amigo/a: ¡Interesante! Yo estoy estudiando también.

Tú: ______________________________

Amigo/a: ¿Cuál asignatura estás estudiando?

Tú: ______________________________

Amigo/a: ¿Te gusta estudiar los viernes?

Tú: ______________________________

Amigo/a: ¿Cuántas horas estudias cada día?

Tú: ______________________________

Amigo/a: ¿Cuál asignatura no te gusta estudiar?

Tú: ______________________________

Amigo/a: ¿De veras? ¿Usas tú el internet cuando estudias?

Tú: ______________________________

Amigo/a: ¿Estudias tú con tus amigos en la escuela?

Tú: ______________________________

VIEJO SAN JUAN

Sección III Total = 20 Puntos

Dominica

SECCIÓN IV

COMPRENSIÓN DE LECTURA (READING COMPREHENSION)
RESPONDE A CADA PREGUNTA (ANSWER ALL QUESTIONS)

4. Lee la siguiente selección con cuidado y responde a las preguntas en INGLÉS.

Read the following selection carefully. Do NOT translate but answer the questions in ENGLISH.

YOU WILL BE PENALIZED FOR DISREGARDING THESE INSTRUCTIONS.

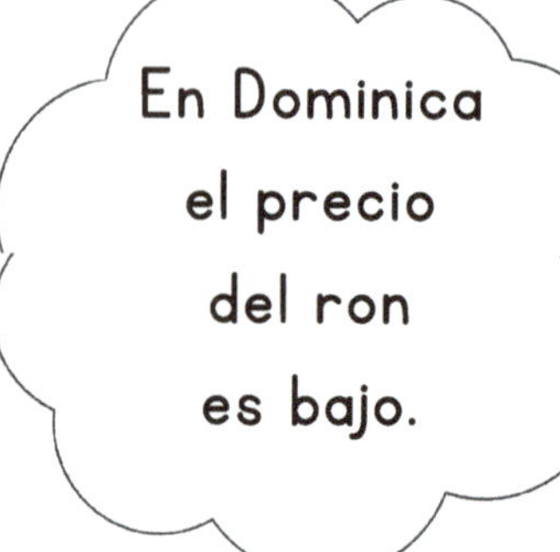

Shopping in Dominica

Dominica (no la República Dominicana) es un país caribeño donde inglés es la lengua oficial. Es un país pequeño pero ir de compras allí es una experiencia excelente. No necesitas tener mucho dinero para comprar muchos productos. Los precios del ron, el café, el perfume y la ropa son bajos. Hay muchos recuerdos* únicos que puedes comprar en la isla como la cerámica y las cestas.

¿Pero dónde puedes comprar estos productos excelentes de alta calidad*? Roseau es el mejor lugar para ir de compras en Dominica. Durante la semana puedes ir de compras desde las ocho de la mañana hasta las cinco de la tarde. También, hay un mercado de vegetales cada miércoles, viernes y sábado. Es más díficil ir de compras los domingos porque muchas tiendas están cerradas. Si quieres, puedes comprar productos caros como las joyas y el cigarro.

(142 palabras)

***recuerdos – souvenirs**
***calidad – quality**

Answer the questions in ENGLISH, based on the selection above. Use a complete sentence for each response.

(a) What is first mentioned about Dominica? **(1 punto)**

____

(b) How is shopping in Dominica described? **(2 puntos)**

____

(c) What does the passage say about a lot of money? (2 puntos)

____

(d) List THREE (3) items that are sold cheaply. (3 puntos)

____

(e) What are some unique souvenirs that are sold there? (2 puntos)

____

(f) Where is the best place in Dominica to go shopping? (1 punto)

____

(g) When are the stores open? (2 puntos)

____

(h) What is said about the vegetable market? (3 puntos)

____

(i) Why is it hard to shop on a Sunday? (2 puntos)

____

(j) Which TWO (2) goods can be expensive? (2 puntos)

____

Sección IV Total = 20 Puntos

TOTAL PUNTOS POR PRUEBA = 100
FIN DE PRUEBA (END OF TEST)
REVISA TU TRABAJO POR FAVOR (PLEASE CHECK YOUR WORK)

PUERTO RICO (RICH PORT)

PIÑA COLADA

MOFONGO

VIEJO SAN JUAN

PAPEL ADICIONAL/NO FALTA NADA DE ESTA PÁGINA

(EXTRA PAPER)/(NOTHING IS MISSING FROM THIS PAGE)

Term 3

NICARAGUA

CÓRDOBA (MONEY)

CAFÉ EN GRANO (COFFEE BEANS)

EL LAGO DE MANAGUA

No cometas los mismos errores

(Don't make the same mistakes)

Below are common mistakes made by students of Spanish. Please note the mistakes and the corrections given. By avoiding these mistakes, you will be sure to improve your writing skills in Spanish.

LA GRAMÁTICA (GRAMMAR)		
Inglés	**Español con error**	**Español correcto**
1. I read books.	Yo leer los libros.	Yo leo los libros.
2. I prefer chocolates.	Mi prefiero chocolates.	Yo prefiero chocolates.
3. I am studying Spanish.	Yo soy estudiar español.	Yo estoy estudiando español.
4. I brush my teeth every day.	Cepillo los dientes cada día.	Me cepillo los dientes cada día.
5. She and I ride a bicycle.	Ella y yo montamos a bicicleta.	Ella y yo montamos en bicicleta.

LA ORTOGRAFÍA (SPELLING)		
Inglés	**Español con error**	**Español correcto**
1. I prefer to play games.	Yo preffiero jugar los juegos.	Yo prefiero jugar los juegos.
2. I'm speaking on the phone.	Estoy hablando por teléphono.	Estoy hablando por teléfono.
3. I want to go to the mall.	Quiero ir al centro commercial.	Quiero ir al centro comercial.
4. I get up at 6 a.m.	Me lavanto a las seis de la mañana.	Me levanto a las seis de la mañana.
5. Dear Ana...	Quierda Ana...	Querida Ana...

EL ORDEN DE LAS PALABRAS (WORD ORDER)		
Inglés	**Español con error**	**Español correcto**
1. What are you doing?	¿Qué estás tú haciendo?	¿Qué estás haciendo tú?
2. I'm washing my dirty clothes.	Estoy lavando mi sucia ropa.	Estoy lavando mi ropa sucia.
3. I think that it's not important.	Pienso que es no importante.	Pienso que no es importante.
4. I speak Spanish well.	Hablo español bien.	Hablo bien español. *

*PLACING BIEN AND MAL WITH RESPECT TO THE VERB DIFFERS IN SPANISH FROM ENGLISH.

Respuestas Abiertas (Free Response)

Nombre:_____________________________ Apellido: ________________________

Clase:______________________________ Profesor/a: ______________________

Fecha: ____

Duración: 90 minutos

INSTRUCCIONES

1. **Esta prueba tiene CUATRO (4) secciones. Responde a cada pregunta en este papel.**

   This test has FOUR (4) sections. Answer all questions on this paper.

2. **Sección I: Tiene DIEZ (10) situaciones. Responde a cada situación en ESPAÑOL.**

   Section I: Has TEN (10) situations. Respond to each in SPANISH.

3. **Sección II: Tiene una carta informal. Escribe la carta en ESPAÑOL.**

   Section II: Has an informal letter. Write the letter in SPANISH.

4. **Sección III: Tiene un diálogo. Rellena los espacios en ESPAÑOL.**

   Section III: Has a dialogue. Complete the dialogue in SPANISH.

5. **Sección IV: Tiene una comprensión de lectura. Responde a las DIEZ (10) preguntas en INGLÉS.**

   Section IV: Has a reading comprehension. Answer the TEN (10) questions in ENGLISH.

SECCIÓN I

LAS SITUACIONES ESCRITAS (WRITTEN SITUATIONS)
RESPONDE A CADA SITUACIÓN (RESPOND TO EACH SITUATION)

1. Write in SPANISH the information required by each of the situations given below. Do NOT write more than ONE sentence for each situation. For some situations, a complete sentence may not be necessary. Write each answer in the space provided.

(a) Your Salvadorian neighbour sends you a text message asking you what you do in the nights. What do you reply?

(3 puntos)

____

(b) Some students are doing a survey in Spanish and ask you to write whether you prefer Apple or Samsung phones. What sentence do you write?

(3 puntos)

____

(c) A Nicaraguan student sends you an email asking if there is a museum in your country. Reply to the email in a sentence.

(3 puntos)

____

(d) You receive a message on *WhatsApp* in Spanish asking where you are going tomorrow. What do you reply?

(3 puntos)

____

(e) Your Spanish teacher has asked all students to write which country they want to visit. What sentence do you write?

(3 puntos)

____

(f) It is your teacher's birthday. Send a message to your classmate who loves Spanish and tell him/her what you are going to buy.

(3 puntos)

____

(g) You want to know if your Cuban friend likes to go to restaurants. What do you ask in the message you send on *Instagram*?

(3 puntos)

____

(h) Your Panamanian friend has sent you a message asking you what you drink with your lunch. What do you reply?

(3 puntos)

____

(i) Your friend from Equatorial Guinea wants to know something you do every day after school. What do you reply on *Twitter*?

(3 puntos)

____

(j) Your Puerto Rican friend sends you a picture of his/her new pet and asks what you think about it. What do you reply in the message you send?

(3 puntos)

____

Sección I Total = 30 Puntos

NICARAGUA

CÓRDOBA (MONEY)

CAFÉ EN GRANO (COFFEE BEANS)

EL LAGO DE MANAGUA

LA CARTA INFORMAL (INFORMAL LETTER)
ESCRIBE UNA CARTA EN ESPAÑOL (WRITE A LETTER IN SPANISH)

2. **Using the following outline as a guide, write a letter in SPANISH of no more than 50 – 60 words.**

YOU WILL BE PENALIZED FOR DISREGARDING THESE INSTRUCTIONS.

Your Guatemalan friend has sent you a letter about his/her morning routine before he/she goes to school. Write him/her a letter about your morning routine. Include:

(i) those with whom you live
(ii) some activities you do in the mornings
(iii) the times when you do some of the activities
(iv) what you eat in the mornings

____

____

____

____

____

____

____

____

____

____

____

____

____

____

(Do NOT write your real name and address, but include the date in Spanish and use the appropriate beginning and ending.)

Sección II Total = 30 Puntos

SECCIÓN III

EL DIÁLOGO CONTEXTUAL (CONTEXTUAL DIALOGUE)
LEE Y RELLENA EL DIÁLOGO EN ESPAÑOL
(READ AND COMPLETE THE DIALOGUE IN SPANISH)

NICARAGUA

CÓRDOBA (MONEY)

CAFÉ EN GRANO (COFFEE BEANS)

3. Use 50 – 60 words to complete the dialogue between you and Enrique Iglesias (a Spanish musician), giving your responses in SPANISH.

You have listened to Enrique Iglesias' new song and decide to message him on *Facebook*. Complete the dialogue you have with him and include:

(i) your wellbeing
(ii) your favourite song
iii) when you normally listen to music
(iv) popular type of music in your country
(v) number of hours you listen to music

Responses to ALL the cues provided must be included in the completed dialogue.

Tú: ¡Hola, Enrique! ¿Cómo estás?

Enrique: Estoy muy bien, ¿y tú?

Tú: ______________________________

Enrique: ¿Te gusta la música?

Tú: ______________________________

Enrique: ¿Escuchas la música en español?

Tú: ______________________________

Enrique: ¿Cuál es tu canción favorita?

Tú: ______________________________

Enrique: ¿Normalmente cuándo escuchas la música?

Tú: ______________________________

Enrique: ¿Cuál prefieres: la música en inglés o la música en español?

Tú: ______________________________

Enrique: Yo también. ¿Qué tipo de música es popular en tu país?

Tú: ______________________________

Enrique: ¿Cuántas horas al día escuchas la música?

Tú: ______________________________

Enrigue: Bueno. Para mí, la música es muy importante. Hasta luego.

Tú: ______________________________

EL LAGO DE MANAGUA

Sección III Total = 20 Puntos

SECCIÓN IV

COMPRENSIÓN DE LECTURA (READING COMPREHENSION)
RESPONDE A CADA PREGUNTA (ANSWER ALL QUESTIONS)

4. Lee la siguiente selección con cuidado y responde a las preguntas en INGLÉS.

Read the following selection carefully. Do NOT translate but answer the questions in ENGLISH.

YOU WILL BE PENALIZED FOR DISREGARDING THESE INSTRUCTIONS.

Let's talk Antiguan Creole

La lengua oficial de Antigua y Barbuda es inglés pero muchas personas en el país hablan el criollo. El criollo no es oficial pero es una lengua bonita que tiene la influencia de la Gran Bretaña y el oeste de África. Otros países caribeños tienen la influencia en el criollo de Antigua. Dos palabras africanas que se usan en el criollo de Antigua son, *nyam,* un verbo que significa *comer*, y *gee*, un verbo que significa *dar*.

Porque más y más personas de varios países caribeños ahora viven en Antigua, usualmente puedes escuchar el criollo de varios países allí. En el criollo de Antigua se usan palabras como, *breda* que significa 'un buen amigo' y la expresión *'sell off'* que significa que algo es excelente. El criollo maravilloso de Antigua es una representación de la historia y la cultura del país.

(141 palabras)

Answer the questions in ENGLISH, based on the selection above. Use a complete sentence for each response.

(a) What is the official language of Antigua and Barbuda? **(1 punto)**

____

(b) How is Antiguan creole described? **(2 puntos)**

____

(c) Which regions influence Antiguan creole? **(2 puntos)**

____

(d) What is said about Caribbean countries? **(3 puntos)**

____

(e) What are two African words used in Antiguan creole? **(2 puntos)**

____

(f) What do these two African words mean? **(2 puntos)**

____

(g) Why can you hear creole words from other countries in Antigua? **(2 puntos)**

____

(h) What is *'breda'*? **(2 puntos)**

____

(i) What does *'sell off'* mean in the passage? **(2 puntos)**

____

(j) What does Antiguan creole represent? **(2 puntos)**

____

Sección IV Total = 20 Puntos

TOTAL PUNTOS POR PRUEBA = 100
FIN DE PRUEBA (END OF TEST)
REVISA TU TRABAJO POR FAVOR (PLEASE CHECK YOUR WORK)

NICARAGUA

CÓRDOBA (MONEY)

CAFÉ EN GRANO (COFFEE BEANS)

EL LAGO DE MANAGUA

PAPEL ADICIONAL/NO FALTA NADA DE ESTA PÁGINA

(EXTRA PAPER)/(NOTHING IS MISSING FROM THIS PAGE)

Term 3

ARGENTINA
(SILVERY/ LAND BESIDE THE SILVERY RIVER)

TANGO

ASADO

FÚTBOL (FOOTBALL)

No cometas los mismos errores

(Don't make the same mistakes)

Below are common mistakes made by students of Spanish. Please note the mistakes and the corrections given. By avoiding these mistakes, you will be sure to improve your writing skills in Spanish.

PUNTUACIÓN Y MAYÚSCULAS (PUNCTUATION AND CAPITALIZATION)		
Inglés	**Español con error**	**Español correcto**
1. I want to go to the beach on Sunday.	Quiero ir a la playa el Domingo.	Quiero ir a la playa el domingo.
2. She and I prefer ice cream.	Ella y Yo preferimos el helado.	Ella y yo preferimos el helado.
3. What do you want to do?	Qué quieres hacer?	¿Qué quieres hacer?
4. I'm washing, cooking, and listening to music.	Estoy lavando, limpiando, y escuchando la música.	Estoy lavando, cocinando, y escuchando la música.
5. I want to sleep!	Quiero dormir!	¡Quiero dormir!

LETRAS CON TILDES (LETTERS WITH TILDES)		
Inglés	**Español con error**	**Español correcto**
1. I bathe at 6:00 a.m.	Me bano a las seis de la mañana.	Me baño a las seis de la mañana.
2. What I like most is reading.	Lo que mas me gusta es leer.	Lo que más me gusta es leer.
3. I want to watch a movie!	¡Quiero mirar una pelicula!	¡Quiero mirar una película!
4. Caringly/ affectionately	Con carino	Con cariño
5. Yes, I prefer to drink water.	Si, prefiero beber el agua.	Sí, prefiero beber el agua.

EL VOCABULARIO (VOCABULARY)		
Inglés	**Español con error**	**Español correcto**
1. What do you think?	¿Cuál piensas tú?	¿Qué piensas tú?
2. I watch a movie.	Yo reloj una película.	Yo miro la película.
3. At what time do you brush your teeth?	¿A qué tiempo te cepillas los dientes?	¿A qué hora te cepillas los dientes?
4. They are washing the car.	Ustedes están lavando el carro.	Ellos están lavando el carro.
5. I want to rest because I am tired.	Quiero descansar por qué estoy cansado.	Quiero descansar porque estoy cansado.

Respuestas Abiertas (Free Response)

Nombre:____________________________ Apellido: ________________________

Clase:_____________________________ Profesor/a: ______________________

Fecha: ____

Duración: 90 minutos

INSTRUCCIONES

1. **Esta prueba tiene CUATRO (4) secciones. Responde a cada pregunta en este papel.**

   This test has FOUR (4) sections. Answer all questions on this paper.

2. **Sección I: Tiene DIEZ (10) situaciones. Responde a cada situación en ESPAÑOL.**

   Section I: Has TEN (10) situations. Respond to each in SPANISH.

3. **Sección II: Tiene una carta informal. Escribe la carta en ESPAÑOL.**

   Section II: Has an informal letter. Write the letter in SPANISH.

4. **Sección III: Tiene un diálogo. Rellena los espacios en ESPAÑOL.**

   Section III: Has a dialogue. Complete the dialogue in SPANISH.

5. **Sección IV: Tiene una comprensión de lectura. Responde a las DIEZ (10) preguntas en INGLÉS.**

   Section IV: Has a reading comprehension. Answer the TEN (10) questions in ENGLISH.

Ecuador

SECCIÓN I

LAS SITUACIONES ESCRITAS (WRITTEN SITUATIONS)
RESPONDE A CADA SITUACIÓN (RESPOND TO EACH SITUATION)

1. **Write in SPANISH the information required by each of the situations given below. Do NOT write more than ONE sentence for each situation. For some situations, a complete sentence may not be necessary. Write each answer in the space provided.**

(a) You go to a library in Panama and fill out a survey before leaving. What comment do you write about the place?

(3 puntos)

____

(b) You want to know the time your Guatemalan friend does something. What do you ask in the message you send him/her?

(3 puntos)

____

(c) Your friend from the Dominican Republic is hosting a big event today. What message do you send him/her on *Twitter*?

(3 puntos)

____

(d) You want your relative's permission to do something. Since he/she speaks Spanish, what do you ask in the message you send him/her?

(3 puntos)

____

(e) You are unable to do something for your Argentinian friend. Send a message to him/her telling him/her this.

(3 puntos)

____

(f) A Spanish company is doing an online survey to find out what teenagers do on their cellphones. What do you reply?

(3 puntos)

___

(g) While at school you receive a text message from your Nicaraguan pen pal asking what you and your friends are doing. What do you reply?

(3 puntos)

___

(h) You receive an email from your Paraguayan friend asking you when you are going to visit his/her country. What do you reply in your message?

(3 puntos)

___

(i) Your classmate sends a message in the Spanish *WhatsApp* group asking what Mexican food students want to eat. What do you reply?

(3 puntos)

___

(j) You just got some news. Send an email to your Cuban classmate telling him/her how you feel.

(3 puntos)

___

Sección I Total = 30 Puntos

LA CARTA INFORMAL (INFORMAL LETTER)
ESCRIBE UNA CARTA EN ESPAÑOL (WRITE A LETTER IN SPANISH)

2. **Using the following outline as a guide, write a letter in SPANISH of no more than 50 – 60 words.**

   YOU WILL BE PENALIZED FOR DISREGARDING THESE INSTRUCTIONS.

   You are going on a school trip tomorrow. Write a letter to your Costa Rican friend in which you include the following:

   (i) where you are going and when
   (ii) information about the place
   (iii) what you are going to do there
   (iv) what you are going to wear

(Do NOT write your real name and address, but include the date in Spanish and use the appropriate beginning and ending.)

Sección II Total = 30 Puntos

SECCIÓN III

EL DIÁLOGO CONTEXTUAL (CONTEXTUAL DIALOGUE)
LEE Y RELLENA EL DIÁLOGO EN ESPAÑOL
(READ AND COMPLETE THE DIALOGUE IN SPANISH)

ARGENTINA
(SILVERY/ LAND BESIDE THE SILVERY RIVER)

TANGO

3. Use 50 – 60 words to complete the dialogue between you and Amanda, a Mexican Party Planner, giving your responses in SPANISH.

You are going to have a party with a Mexican theme soon, so you contact Amanda, a famous Mexican Party Planner on *Instagram*. Complete the dialogue you have with her and include:

(i) greeting and identification
(ii) type of food you want at the party
(iii) number of guests
(iv) what you are going to wear
(v) location of party

Responses to ALL the cues provided must be included in the completed dialogue.

Amanda: Hola. Me llamo Amanda. Encantada. ¿Cuándo es la fiesta?

Tú: ____________________

Amanda: Bueno. ¿Qué comida quieres en tu fiesta?

Tú: ____________________

Amanda: ¿Prefieres el helado de chocolate o el helado de vainilla?

Tú: ____________________

Amanda: ¿Cuál necesitas: jugo de frutas, la limonada o el agua?

Tú: ____________________

Amanda: ¿Quieres una piñata?

Tú: ____________________

Amanda: ¿Cuántas personas vas a invitar a la fiesta?

Tú: ____________________

Amanda: ¿Vas a llevar un poncho y un sombrero?

Tú: ____________________

Amanda: ¿Quieres la fiesta en tu casa o en un hotel?

Tú: ____________________

Amanda: ¿Necesitas la música mexicana?

Tú: ____________________

Amanda: Bueno. Muchas gracias. Hasta mañana.

Tú: ____________________

ASADO

FÚTBOL (FOOTBALL)

Sección III Total = 20 Puntos

SECCIÓN IV

COMPRENSIÓN DE LECTURA (READING COMPREHENSION)
RESPONDE A CADA PREGUNTA (ANSWER ALL QUESTIONS)

4. **Lee la siguiente selección con cuidado y responde a las preguntas en INGLÉS.**

Read the following selection carefully. Do NOT translate but answer the questions in ENGLISH.

YOU WILL BE PENALIZED FOR DISREGARDING THESE INSTRUCTIONS.

Celebrating Caribbean Art

Alrededor del Caribe hay muchos museos donde hay muchos de los mejores artes por los mejores artistas de la región. Estos artes incluyen temas como la política, la identidad, la naturaleza y la cultura. También, el arte caribeño refleja miles de años de su historia. Hoy, puedes encontrar el arte de los Taínos, los Caribes y los Kalinago. El arte caribeño es una combinación de muchas culturas como las de África, Europa y Asia.

Unos nombres populares en el mundo del arte en el Caribe son Hector Hyppolite, un pintor haitiano; Edna Manley, una escultora* jamaicana y Jorge Severino de la República Dominicana. Muchas de las pinturas* más populares de Severino son imágenes de una mujer negra y hermosa con una sola flor roja en el pelo. Normalmente estas mujeres llevan vestidos blancos y joyas lujosas. La galería de arte dominicana tiene una colección grande del arte de Severino.

(149 palabras)

***escultor/a – sculptor**
***pintura(s) – painting(s)**

Answer the questions in ENGLISH, based on the selection above. Use a complete sentence for each response.

(a) What can be found in museums in the Caribbean? **(2 puntos)**

____

(b) Identify THREE (3) themes that can be found in Caribbean art. **(3 puntos)**

____

(c) What does Caribbean art reflect? (2 puntos)

___

(d) Which TWO (2) historic groups' art can be found in the Caribbean? (2 puntos)

___

(e) Name ONE (1) region that influences Caribbean art. (1 punto)

___

(f) Who was Hector Hyppolite? (2 puntos)

___

(g) What was Edna Manley's job? (1 punto)

___

(h) What are the nationalities of Edna Manley and Jorge Severino? (2 puntos)

___

(i) Describe the typical woman Severino paints. (3 puntos)

___

(j) What is said about the Dominican Republic art gallery? (2 puntos)

___

Sección IV Total = 20 Puntos

TOTAL PUNTOS POR PRUEBA = 100
FIN DE PRUEBA (END OF TEST)
REVISA TU TRABAJO POR FAVOR (PLEASE CHECK YOUR WORK)

ARGENTINA
(SILVERY/ LAND BESIDE THE SILVERY RIVER)

TANGO

ASADO

FÚTBOL (FOOTBALL)

PAPEL ADICIONAL/NO FALTA NADA DE ESTA PÁGINA

(EXTRA PAPER)/(NOTHING IS MISSING FROM THIS PAGE)

(Ninth Grade)

Term 1 (Septiembre – Diciembre)

1. Revision
2. Vacation
3. Travelling
4. What do you have to do?
5. Commands
6. Comparison
7. At the hotel
8. Ordinal numbers (1st to 10th)
9. Do you know (how to)?

Term 2 (Enero – Marzo/Abril)

1. What did you do?
2. Preferred activities
3. I liked/disliked it
4. Sports and recreation
5. What happened?
6. How did you do that?
7. Did you enjoy yourself?

Term 3 (Abril/Mayo – Junio)

1. Where I went
2. A day at the mall
3. What I had to do
4. I arrived late
5. Restaurant (2)
6. I hope to...
7. Shopping at the market

GRADE 9/ THIRD FORM

Funciones Comunicativas		Communicative Functions
Term 1	**Term 2**	**Term 3**
1. **Comparing-** (a) (noun/pronoun) es más (adjective) que ... Paul es más alto que Pedro (b) (noun/pronoun) es tan (adjective) como ...Ana es tan bonita como Linda	1. **Enquiring about past events -** ¿Qué hiciste?/ ¿Cuándo comenzó?/ ¿Dónde compraste ...? etc.	1. **Asking about goods when shopping -** ¿Es barato/a caro/a? / ¿Qué talla llevas? / ¿Qué número calzas?
2. **Expressing commands/ instructions –** Hay que + verb/ Debes + verb/ !Para! etc. Hay que estudiar	2. **Expressing past actions –** (Yo) comí, (Yo) viajé / (Yo) estudié etc.	2. **Expressing hope –** (Yo) espero + verb. Eg. Espero ir a la universidad/ Espero recibir buenas notas.
3. **Expressing spare-time activities –** Yo nado/ Yo leo/ Yo bailo/ Yo escucho la música	3. **Expressing thoughts on sports** – (Yo) pienso que los deportes son... porque...	3. **Inviting –** Te invito / Voy a invitar a ...
4. **Providing reasons for doing something** – Es necesario porque/ Es importante porque etc.	4. **Indicating pleasure and displeasure in the past –** No me gustó/ No me gustaron/ No le gustó etc.	4. **Ordering a meal –** Me gustaría... / ¿Puedo ver el menú de postres?
5. **Suggesting** – Hay que + verb/ Debes + verb/ Tienes que + verb	5. **Outlining preferred activities –** Prefiero montar en bicicleta/ Prefiero jugar a los videojuegos/ Prefiero navegar por la red.	5. **Outlining reasons for lateness –** (Yo) llegué tarde porque... / (Yo) vine tarde porque... / No pude venir temprano porque...
6. **Wishing a safe journey –** Buen viaje		

ECUADOR
(EQUATOR)

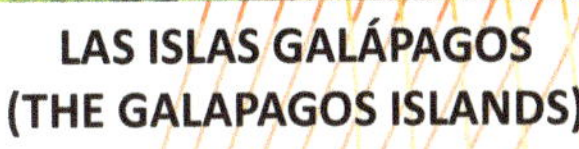
LAS ISLAS GALÁPAGOS
(THE GALAPAGOS ISLANDS)

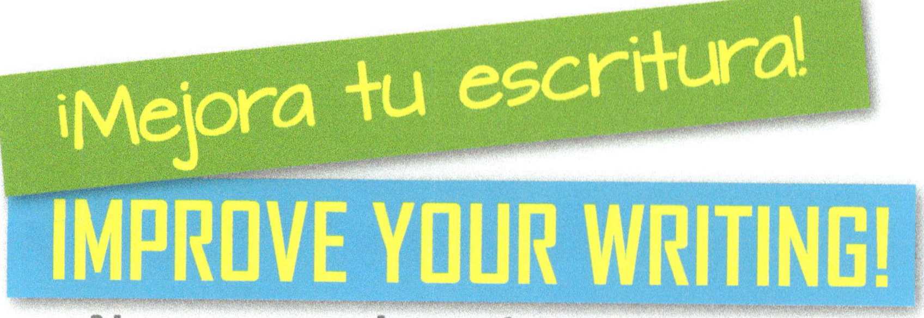

No cometas los mismos errores
(Don't make the same mistakes)

Below are common mistakes made by students of Spanish. Please note the mistakes and the corrections given. By avoiding these mistakes, you will be sure to improve your writing skills in Spanish.

LA GRAMÁTICA (GRAMMAR)		
Inglés	**Español con error**	**Español correcto**
1. I have to clean my room.	Tengo limpiar mi dormitorio.	Tengo que limpiar mi dormitorio.
2. Study your Spanish book!	¡Estudias tu libro de español!	¡Estudia tu libro de español!
3. John is taller than Mary.	Juan es más alta que María.	Juan es más alto que María.
4. I am at the hotel now.	Estoy al hotel ahora.	Estoy en el hotel ahora.
5. She is the second daughter.	Ella es el segundo hija.	Ella es la segunda hija.

LA ORTOGRAFÍA (SPELLING)		
Inglés	**Español con error**	**Español correcto**
1. I travel by bus.	Yo viaho por autobús.	Yo viajo por autobús.
2. I have to attend school.	Tengo que assistir al colegio.	Tengo que asistir al colegio.
3. We are on the fourth floor.	Estamos en el quarto piso.	Estamos en el cuarto piso.
4. I'm going on vacation today.	Me voy de vacatión hoy.	Me voy de vacación hoy.
5. The hotel has many attractions.	El hotel tiene muchas attraciones.	El hotel tiene muchas atracciones.

EL ORDEN DE LAS PALABRAS (WORD ORDER)		
Inglés	**Español con error**	**Español correcto**
1. Colombia is a beautiful country.	Colombia es un hermoso país.	Colombia es un país hermoso.
2. When are we going on vacation?	¿Cuándo nosotros vamos de vacación?	¿Cuándo vamos nosotros de vacación?
3. I don't know!	¡No yo sé!	¡Yo no sé!
4. December 4, 2024.	Diciembre 4, 2024.	4 de diciembre de 2024.

Respuestas Abiertas (Free Response)

Nombre:__________________________ Apellido: ______________________

Clase:___________________________ Profesor/a: _____________________

Fecha: ____

Duración: 90 minutos

INSTRUCCIONES

1. **Esta prueba tiene CUATRO (4) secciones. Responde a cada pregunta en este papel.**

   This test has FOUR (4) sections. Answer all questions on this paper.

2. **Sección I: Tiene DIEZ (10) situaciones. Responde a cada situación en ESPAÑOL.**

   Section I: Has TEN (10) situations. Respond to each in SPANISH.

3. **Sección II: Tiene una carta informal. Escribe la carta en ESPAÑOL.**

   Section II: Has an informal letter. Write the letter in SPANISH.

4. **Sección III: Tiene un diálogo. Rellena los espacios en ESPAÑOL.**

   Section III: Has a dialogue. Complete the dialogue in SPANISH.

5. **Sección IV: Tiene una comprensión de lectura. Responde a las DIEZ (10) preguntas en INGLÉS.**

   Section IV: Has a reading comprehension. Answer the TEN (10) questions in ENGLISH.

Nicaragua

SECCIÓN I

LAS SITUACIONES ESCRITAS (WRITTEN SITUATIONS)
RESPONDE A CADA SITUACIÓN (RESPOND TO EACH SITUATION)

1. **Write in SPANISH the information required by each of the situations given below. Do NOT write more than ONE sentence for each situation. For some situations, a complete sentence may not be necessary. Write each answer in the space provided.**

(a) Your Mexican friend sends you a message on *WhatsApp* asking you how you travel to school. What do you reply in the message you send?

(3 puntos)

____

(b) Your Colombian pen pal has sent you a text message asking you to compare two of your relatives. What response do you send in your message?

(3 puntos)

____

(c) You have to do something before you go to the cinema with your Argentinian friend. Send him/her a message explaining what you have to do.

(3 puntos)

____

(d) Your Nicaraguan classmate sends you a note in class asking you where he/she can buy something. What do you reply in the note?

(3 puntos)

____

(e) One of your relatives is learning Spanish and you want him/her to do a chore for you. What do you instruct him/her to do in the message you send?

(3 puntos)

____

(f) You buy a card for your friend from the Dominican Republic who is going back to his/her country. What do you write in the card?

(3 puntos)

____

(g) You want to know what time your Puerto Rican friend's school ends. What do you ask in the message you send him/her on *Instagram*?

(3 puntos)

____

(h) Your Spanish teacher has asked students to write if they know how to cook well. What sentence do you write to reply to his/her question?

(3 puntos)

____

(i) Your Ecuadorian friend wants to know on which floor your class is located at your school. What sentence do you write in the email you send him/her?

(3 puntos)

____

(j) You receive a voice note in very fast Spanish and you cannot understand it. What do you ask the person to do in the *WhatsApp* message you send?

(3 puntos)

____

Sección I Total = 30 Puntos

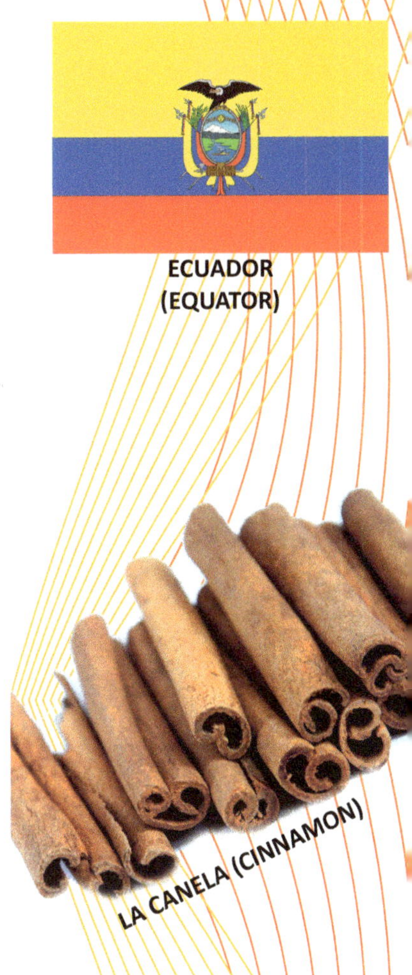

ECUADOR (EQUATOR)

LA CANELA (CINNAMON)

CUY (ROASTED GUINEA PIG)

LAS ISLAS GALÁPAGOS (THE GALAPAGOS ISLANDS)

SECCIÓN II

LA CARTA INFORMAL (INFORMAL LETTER)
ESCRIBE UNA CARTA EN ESPAÑOL (WRITE A LETTER IN SPANISH)

2. Using the following outline as a guide, write a letter in SPANISH of no more than 80 – 100 words.

YOU WILL BE PENALIZED FOR DISREGARDING THESE INSTRUCTIONS.

You and your family are going to a famous hotel for a week and you are very happy. Write a letter to your Chilean friend about this plan. Be sure to include:

(i) when you are going and with whom
(ii) the name of the hotel and how you feel
(iii) what you are going to do there
(iv) some activities for which the hotel is famous

(Do NOT write your real name and address, but include the date in Spanish and use the appropriate beginning and ending.)

Sección II Total = 30 Puntos

SECCIÓN III

EL DIÁLOGO CONTEXTUAL (CONTEXTUAL DIALOGUE)
LEE Y RELLENA EL DIÁLOGO EN ESPAÑOL
(READ AND COMPLETE THE DIALOGUE IN SPANISH)

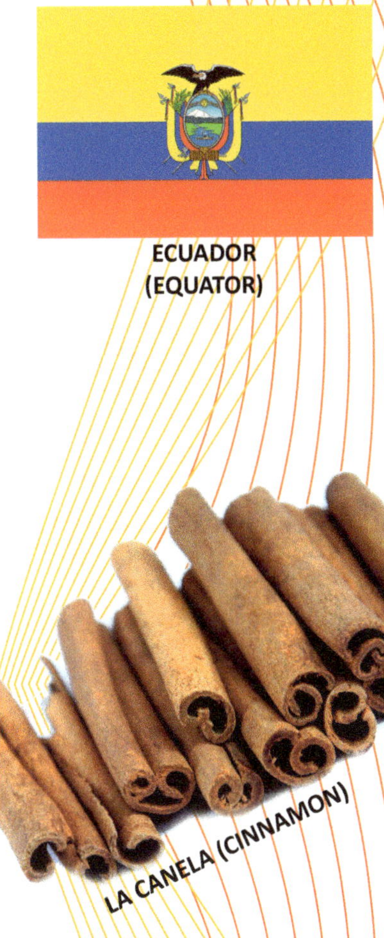
ECUADOR
(EQUATOR)

LA CANELA (CINNAMON)

3. Use 60 – 80 words to complete the dialogue between you and an employee of the Ministry of Education in your country.

The Ministry of Education is having a competition for third form students and you want to win a free trip to any Spanish-speaking country so you answer some questions asked by a worker on the Ministry's website. Be sure to include:

(i) country of interest
(ii) reason for wanting to go there
(iii) how long you want to spend there
(iv) necessary documents
(v) what the country is famous for

Responses to ALL the cues provided must be included in the completed dialogue.

Tú: **¡Hola! Yo quiero ganar un viaje.**
Empleado: ¡Hola! ¿Qué tal y cuál es tu nombre?
Tú: ____________________
Empleado: Mucho gusto. Bueno. ¿Qué país quieres visitar?
Tú: ____________________
Empleado: ¿Y por qué quieres ir a este país?
Tú: ____________________
Empleado: ¡Interesante! ¿Qué tipo de comida es popular allí?
Tú: ____________________
Empleado: ¿En qué mes es mejor ir allí?
Tú: ____________________
Empleado: ¿Cuántos días quieres pasar en este país?
Tú: ____________________
Empleado: ¿Ya tienes amigos allí?
Tú: ____________________
Empleado: ¿Puedes ir allí por barco o solo por avión?
Tú: ____________________
Empleado: ¿Qué documentos necesitas para viajar allí?
Tú: ____________________
Empleado: ¿Qué es más famoso en este país?
Tú: ____________________
Empleado: Bueno. Muchas gracias por responder a las preguntas. Vamos a contactarte pronto.
Tú: ____________________

CUY (ROASTED GUINEA PIG)

LAS ISLAS GALÁPAGOS
(THE GALAPAGOS ISLANDS)

Sección III Total = 20 Puntos

Jamaica

Bob Marley

SECCIÓN IV

COMPRENSIÓN DE LECTURA (READING COMPREHENSION)
RESPONDE A CADA PREGUNTA (ANSWER ALL QUESTIONS)

4. Lee la siguiente selección con cuidado y responde a las preguntas en INGLÉS.

Read the following selection carefully. Do NOT translate but answer the questions in ENGLISH.

YOU WILL BE PENALIZED FOR DISREGARDING THESE INSTRUCTIONS.

Jamaican Music

La música es muy importante en Jamaica. A los jamaicanos les gusta escuchar la música. La música pop de América es popular en Jamaica y también la música soul. Pero, en muchas partes del mundo, muchas personas asocian Jamaica con la música reggae y la música 'Dancehall'. Cuando los jamaicanos escuchan la música, normalmente bailan. Recientemente, en 2018, UNESCO añadió* la música reggae a la lista de patrimonio* cultural.

Bob Marley es el cantante de la música reggae más famoso del mundo. La música de Bob es una inspiración para muchas personas. Bob nació el 6 de febrero de 1945 en Santa Ana. La música reggae comenzó en los años 1960. Beres Hammond es cantante de la música reggae también. La música 'Dancehall' comenzó en los años 1970. Hoy, Beenie Man, Sean Paul y Spice son los cantantes de la música 'Dancehall' más populares.

(142 palabras)

*** añadir – to add**
*** patrimonio – heritage**

Answer the questions in ENGLISH, based on the selection above. Use a complete sentence for each response.

(a) How is music described? **(1 punto)**

____

(b) What do Jamaicans like? **(2 puntos)**

____

(c) Which two (2) types of foreign music are popular in Jamaica? (2 puntos)

____

(d) What is Jamaica usually associated with, to foreigners? (2 puntos)

____

(e) What do Jamaicans often do when they hear music? (2 puntos)

____

(f) Who is Bob Marley according to the passage? (2 puntos)

____

(g) How is Bob Marley's music described? (2 puntos)

____

(h) When and where was Bob Marley born? (2 puntos)

____

(i) When did Reggae and 'Dancehall' music begin? (2 puntos)

____

(j) Name three (3) popular 'Dancehall' artistes mentioned. (3 puntos)

____

Sección IV Total = 20 Puntos

TOTAL PUNTOS POR PRUEBA = 100
FIN DE PRUEBA (END OF TEST)
REVISA TU TRABAJO POR FAVOR (PLEASE CHECK YOUR WORK)

ECUADOR (EQUATOR)

LA CANELA (CINNAMON)

CUY (ROASTED GUINEA PIG)

LAS ISLAS GALÁPAGOS (THE GALAPAGOS ISLANDS)

PAPEL ADICIONAL/NO FALTA NADA DE ESTA PÁGINA

(EXTRA PAPER)/(NOTHING IS MISSING FROM THIS PAGE)

Grade 9

Term 1

PRACTICE TEST 2

COLOMBIA
(NAMED AFTER COLUMBUS)

EL ARTE DE BOTERO

VESTIDO TRADICIONAL
(TRADITIONAL DRESS)

LAS ESMERALDAS

No cometas los mismos errores

(Don't make the same mistakes)

Below are common mistakes made by students of Spanish. Please note the mistakes and the corrections given. By avoiding these mistakes, you will be sure to improve your writing skills in Spanish.

PUNTUACIÓN Y MAYÚSCULAS (PUNCTUATION AND CAPITALIZATION)		
Inglés	**Español con error**	**Español correcto**
1. The holiday starts on Monday.	La vacación comienza el Lunes.	La vacación comienza el lunes.
2. The Cubans are very kind.	Los Cubanos son muy generosos.	Los cubanos son muy generosos.
3. Close the door, Marcos!	Cierra la puerta, Marcos!	¡Cierra la puerta, Marcos!
4. Who is shorter, David or Jorge?	Quién es más bajo, David o Jorge?	¿Quién es más bajo, David o Jorge?
5. On the 2nd day, I'm going to...	El 2nd día, voy a ...	El 2.° día, voy a ...

LETRAS CON TILDES (LETTERS WITH TILDES)		
Inglés	**Español con error**	**Español correcto**
1. I know her name.	Yo se su nombre.	Yo sé su nombre.
2. The hotel has a water slide.	El hotel tiene un tobogan acuatico.	El hotel tiene un tobogán acuático.
3. It's a Caribbean island.	Es una isla caribena.	Es una isla caribeña.
4. French is easier than Spanish.	Francés es más facíl que español.	Francés es más fácil que español.
5. I have to accompany my family.	Tengo que acompanar a mi familia.	Tengo que acompañar a mi familia.

EL VOCABULARIO (VOCABULARY)		
Inglés	**Español con error**	**Español correcto**
1. Wash the dishes!	¡Lleva los platos!	¡Lava los platos!
2. I don't know Andrés.	No sé a Andrés.	No conozco a Andrés.
3. I'm going to the countryside.	Voy al país.	Voy al campo.
4. I want to see the exotic scenery.	Quiero mirar la vista exótica.	Quiero ver la vista exótica.
5. I have to go to the stadium.	Tengo que ir al estudio.	Tengo que ir al estadio.

Respuestas Abiertas (Free Response)

Nombre:______________________________ Apellido: ________________________

Clase:_______________________________ Profesor/a: _______________________

Fecha: ____

Duración: 90 minutos

INSTRUCCIONES

1. **Esta prueba tiene CUATRO (4) secciones. Responde a cada pregunta en este papel.**

   This test has FOUR (4) sections. Answer all questions on this paper.

2. **Sección I: Tiene DIEZ (10) situaciones. Responde a cada situación en ESPAÑOL.**

   Section I: Has TEN (10) situations. Respond to each in SPANISH.

3. **Sección II: Tiene una carta informal. Escribe la carta en ESPAÑOL.**

   Section II: Has an informal letter. Write the letter in SPANISH.

4. **Sección III: Tiene un diálogo. Rellena los espacios en ESPAÑOL.**

   Section III: Has a dialogue. Complete the dialogue in SPANISH.

5. **Sección IV: Tiene una comprensión de lectura. Responde a las DIEZ (10) preguntas en INGLÉS.**

   Section IV: Has a reading comprehension. Answer the TEN (10) questions in ENGLISH.

Machu Picchu, Peru

SECCIÓN I

LAS SITUACIONES ESCRITAS (WRITTEN SITUATIONS)
RESPONDE A CADA SITUACIÓN (RESPOND TO EACH SITUATION)

1. Write in SPANISH the information required by each of the situations given below. Do NOT write more than ONE sentence for each situation. For some situations, a complete sentence may not be necessary. Write each answer in the space provided.

(a) Your friend at another school who studies Spanish said he/she does not see the reason to study Spanish. Send him/her an email giving him/her one reason.

(3 puntos)

____

(b) Your Guatemalan friend sends you a message on *Messenger* asking you when you are going on vacation. What sentence do you write to explain this?

(3 puntos)

____

(c) You want to know who does a specific chore in your Peruvian friend's house. What do you ask him/her in the message you send on *WhatsApp*?

(3 puntos)

____

(d) While on vacation you take a picture of something and post it on *Instagram*. What comment do you put below the picture in Spanish?

(3 puntos)

____

(e) The Spanish club is translating school rules into Spanish for the new students. Write one of the rules that you will put on the notice board.

(3 puntos)

____

(f) Your Bolivian friend has sent you a message saying that he/she is failing in school. What do you suggest that he/she needs to do?

(3 puntos)

____

(g) Your Spanish teacher has asked students to state one similarity between two items. What do you write on your paper?

(3 puntos)

____

(h) Your Nicaraguan pen pal sent you a letter asking which classmate you admire and why. What do you reply in your letter to him/her?

(3 puntos)

____

(i) Your school is having a *Quinceañera* for grade nine students and you were asked to design the invitation card. Write one piece of information that you put on the card.

(3 puntos)

____

(j) You are going to a party. Send your Salvadorian friend a message telling him/her one thing that you are going to do to get ready for the party.

(3 puntos)

____

Sección I Total = 30 Puntos

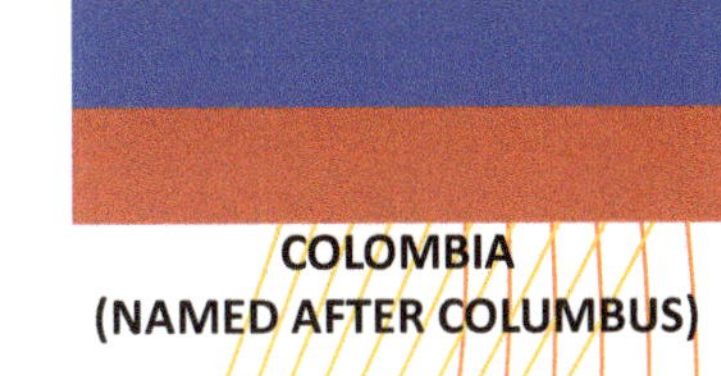

COLOMBIA
(NAMED AFTER COLUMBUS)

EL ARTE DE BOTERO

VESTIDO TRADICIONAL
(TRADITIONAL DRESS)

LAS ESMERALDAS

SECCIÓN II

LA CARTA INFORMAL (INFORMAL LETTER)
ESCRIBE UNA CARTA EN ESPAÑOL (WRITE A LETTER IN SPANISH)

2. Using the following outline as a guide, write a letter in SPANISH of no more than 80 – 100 words.

YOU WILL BE PENALIZED FOR DISREGARDING THESE INSTRUCTIONS.

You are going to receive a lot of money from a relative for a special occasion. Write a letter to your Uruguayan classmate in which you include:

(i) when you are going to receive the money
(ii) how much money you are going to receive and how you feel
(iii) who you are going to get money from and why
(iv) at least THREE (3) things that you are going to do with the money

____

____

____

____

____

____

____

____

____

____

____

____

____

____

(Do NOT write your real name and address, but include the date in Spanish and use the appropriate beginning and ending.)

Sección II Total = 30 Puntos

SECCIÓN III

EL DIÁLOGO CONTEXTUAL (CONTEXTUAL DIALOGUE)
LEE Y RELLENA EL DIÁLOGO EN ESPAÑOL
(READ AND COMPLETE THE DIALOGUE IN SPANISH)

COLOMBIA
(NAMED AFTER COLUMBUS)

3. **Use 60 – 80 words to complete the dialogue between you and your friend from Equatorial Guinea, in Africa.**

Your Spanish-speaking friend from Africa is coming to your country for vacation and wants to spend some time with you. Complete the dialogue you have with him/her online. Include:

(i) where you and your friend can go
(ii) reason for going to this place
(iii) activities available and prices of activities
(iv your family members he/she is going to meet
(v) how long your friend can spend with you

Responses to ALL the cues provided must be included in the completed dialogue.

Amigo/a: ¡Epa! ¿Qué hay?
Tú: ______________________________
Amigo/a Voy a visitar tu país pronto. ¿Podemos irnos juntos?
Tú: ______________________________
Amigo/a: ¿En qué parte del país vives?
Tú: ______________________________
Amigo/a: ¿Adónde podemos ir?
Tú: ______________________________
Amigo/a: ¿Por qué este lugar?
Tú: ______________________________
Amigo/a: ¿Qué actividades podemos hacer allí?
Tú: ______________________________
Amigo/a: ¿Cómo son los precios de las actividades allí?
Tú: ______________________________
Amigo/a: ¿Qué otro lugar podemos visitar?
Tú: ______________________________
Amigo/a: ¡Qué chévere! ¿Quién en tu familia voy a encontrar?
Tú: ______________________________
Amigo/a: ¿De veras? Yo quiero encontrar a tu mamá.
Tú: ______________________________
Amigo/a: ¿Cuántos días puedo pasar contigo?
Tú: ______________________________
Amigo/a: Bueno. Estoy muy emocionado/a de visitarte y tu país.
Tú: ______________________________
Amigo/a: Chao. Hasta la vista.

EL ARTE DE BOTERO

VESTIDO TRADICIONAL
(TRADITIONAL DRESS)

LAS ESMERALDAS

Sección III Total = 20 Puntos

SECCIÓN IV

COMPRENSIÓN DE LECTURA (READING COMPREHENSION)
RESPONDE A CADA PREGUNTA (ANSWER ALL QUESTIONS)

4. Lee la siguiente selección con cuidado y responde a las preguntas en INGLÉS.

Read the following selection carefully. Do NOT translate but answer the questions in ENGLISH.

YOU WILL BE PENALIZED FOR DISREGARDING THESE INSTRUCTIONS.

UNESCO World Heritage Sites in the Caribbean.

Hay veinte sitios de la UNESCO en el Caribe. Doce diferentes países caribeños tienen sitios en la lista de la UNESCO pero Cuba tiene más sitios en la lista que todas las otras islas. En total, Cuba tiene nueve de los veinte sitios de la UNESCO. Unos de los sitios en Cuba son la Habana Vieja y el Castillo de San Pedro de la Roca. Además, países como San Cristóbal y Nevis, Haití y Dominica tienen un sitio del patrimonio mundial de la UNESCO.

Unos de los sitios de la UNESCO son clasificados como sitios culturales y unos son naturales. Pero, unos sitios son ambos culturales y naturales. Por ejemplo, en Jamaica las Montañas Azules y las Montañas de John Crow son sitios mixtos. La Habana Vieja es el sitio del patrimonio mundial de la UNESCO más visitado por turistas en el Caribe. La gente caribeña necesita trabajar juntos para proteger sus sitios culturales y naturales.

(156 palabras)

Answer the questions in ENGLISH, based on the selection above. Use a complete sentence for each response.

(a) How many UNESCO World Heritage sites are in the Caribbean?

(1 punto)

____

(b) How many Caribbean countries have UNESCO sites?

(1 punto)

____

(c) What is said about Cuba? (2 puntos)

____

(d) Which Cuban sites are mentioned? (2 puntos)

____

COLOMBIA
(NAMED AFTER COLUMBUS)

(e) Aside from Cuba, name THREE (3) countries with UNESCO sites. (3 puntos)

____

EL ARTE DE BOTERO

(f) What are the THREE (3) classifications of UNESCO sites? (3 puntos)

____

(g) Which places are mentioned in Jamaica? (2 puntos)

____

VESTIDO TRADICIONAL
(TRADITIONAL DRESS)

(h) How are the Jamaican sites classified? (1 punto)

____

(i) What is said about Old Havana? (2 puntos)

____

(j) What advice is given at the end? (3 puntos)

____

LAS ESMERALDAS

Sección IV Total = 20 Puntos

TOTAL PUNTOS POR PRUEBA = 100
FIN DE PRUEBA (END OF TEST)
REVISA TU TRABAJO POR FAVOR (PLEASE CHECK YOUR WORK)

Las Montañas Azules

La Habana Vieja

Cockpit Country

PAPEL ADICIONAL/NO FALTA NADA DE ESTA PÁGINA

(EXTRA PAPER)/(NOTHING IS MISSING FROM THIS PAGE)

Grade 9

Term 2

PARAGUAY

TERERÉ

HABAS DE SOJA

SALTOS DEL MONDAY

No cometas los mismos errores

(Don't make the same mistakes)

Below are common mistakes made by students of Spanish. Please note the mistakes and the corrections given. By avoiding these mistakes, you will be sure to improve your writing skills in Spanish.

LA GRAMÁTICA (GRAMMAR)		
Inglés	**Español con error**	**Español correcto**
1. Last night, I ate fried chicken.	Anoche, yo como pollo frito.	Anoche, yo comí pollo frito.
2. I liked the food and the games.	Me gustó la comida y los juegos.	Me gustaron la comida y los juegos.
3. I enjoyed chatting and playing.	Disfruté charlando y jugando.	Disfruté charlar y jugar.
4. I like playing games very much.	Me gusta jugar juegos muy mucho.	Me gusta jugar juegos mucho.
5. I did enjoy myself.	Yo hice divertirme.	Yo me divertí.

LA ORTOGRAFÍA (SPELLING)		
Inglés	**Español con error**	**Español correcto**
1. We visited the city.	Visitamos la cuidad.	Visitamos la ciudad.
2. I play basketball.	Yo juego al basketbol.	Yo juego al basquetbol.
3. I think exercise is important.	Yo pienso que el ejercio es importante.	Yo pienso que el ejercicio es importante.
4. Last Monday, I sang at the concert.	El lunes passado, yo canté en el concierto.	El lunes pasado, yo canté en el concierto.
5. I don't play sports.	Yo no juego los diportes.	Yo no juego los deportes.

EL ORDEN DE LAS PALABRAS (WORD ORDER)		
Inglés	**Español con error**	**Español correcto**
1. My favourite activity is dancing.	Mi favorita actividad es bailar.	Mi actividad favorita es bailar.
2. On Sports Day, I ran.	El Deportes Día, yo corrí.	El Día de Deportes, yo corrí.
3. Did he watch the movie?	¿Él miró la película?	¿Miró él la película?
4. We saw historic sites.	Vimos históricos sitios.	Vimos sitios históricos.

Respuestas Abiertas (Free Response)

Nombre:__________________________ Apellido: ______________________

Clase:____________________________ Profesor/a: _____________________

Fecha: ____

Duración: 90 minutos

INSTRUCCIONES

1. **Esta prueba tiene CUATRO (4) secciones. Responde a cada pregunta en este papel.**

   This test has FOUR (4) sections. Answer all questions on this paper.

2. **Sección I: Tiene DIEZ (10) situaciones. Responde a cada situación en ESPAÑOL.**

   Section I: Has TEN (10) situations. Respond to each in SPANISH.

3. **Sección II: Tiene una carta informal. Escribe la carta en ESPAÑOL.**

   Section II: Has an informal letter. Write the letter in SPANISH.

4. **Sección III: Tiene un diálogo. Rellena los espacios en ESPAÑOL.**

   Section III: Has a dialogue. Complete the dialogue in SPANISH.

5. **Sección IV: Tiene una comprensión de lectura. Responde a las DIEZ (10) preguntas en INGLÉS.**

   Section IV: Has a reading comprehension. Answer the TEN (10) questions in ENGLISH.

SECCIÓN I

LAS SITUACIONES ESCRITAS (WRITTEN SITUATIONS)
RESPONDE A CADA SITUACIÓN (RESPOND TO EACH SITUATION)

1. Write in SPANISH the information required by each of the situations given below. Do NOT write more than ONE sentence for each situation. For some situations, a complete sentence may not be necessary. Write each answer in the space provided.

(a) You receive a text message from your Spanish-speaking friend asking you how you travelled to school this morning. What do you reply in your message?

(3 puntos)

____

(b) Your Argentinian friend has sent you a message online asking you what your favourite activity is. What do you reply?

(3 puntos)

____

(c) Your Guatemalan friend wants to know what you and your school-mates wear to school. What do you tell him/her in the message you send on *Twitter*?

(3 puntos)

____

(d) One night, your Colombian friend made a post on *Facebook* asking people what they ate for dinner. What sentence do you write to reply to the post?

(3 puntos)

____

(e) Your friend who loves Spanish sent you a note in class asking you one thing you did yesterday. What do you reply in the note?

(3 puntos)

____

(f) Your Venezuelan friend sent you a message asking you what you studied last night. What sentence do you write to reply to his/her message?

(3 puntos)

____

(g) You want to know something specific about a recent purchase by your Costa Rican friend. What do you ask in the message you send him/her?

(3 puntos)

____

(h) Your relative who studied in Cuba asked you in a tweet what you received for your last birthday. What do you reply in a tweet that you send?

(3 puntos)

____

(i) You did not do something your Spanish friend asked you to do last week. Send him/her a message explaining this by mentioning what you did not do.

(3 puntos)

____

(j) You are filling out a visa application form to visit a Spanish-speaking country and one question asks where you were born. What do you reply?

(3 puntos)

____

Sección I Total = 30 Puntos

PARAGUAY

TERERÉ

HABAS DE SOJA

SALTOS DEL MONDAY

SECCIÓN II

LA CARTA INFORMAL (INFORMAL LETTER)
ESCRIBE UNA CARTA EN ESPAÑOL (WRITE A LETTER IN SPANISH)

2. **Using the following outline as a guide, write a letter in SPANISH of no more than 80 – 100 words.**

   YOU WILL BE PENALIZED FOR DISREGARDING THESE INSTRUCTIONS.

   You recently had a wonderful weekend doing many things. Write a letter to your Panamanian friend about the weekend in which you include:

   (i) a place you visited and with whom
   (ii) some activities you and your friends did
   (iii) what you bought and ate
   (iv) what you saw

(Do NOT write your real name and address, but include the date in Spanish and use the appropriate beginning and ending.)

Sección II Total = 30 Puntos

SECCIÓN III

EL DIÁLOGO CONTEXTUAL (CONTEXTUAL DIALOGUE)
LEE Y RELLENA EL DIÁLOGO EN ESPAÑOL
(READ AND COMPLETE THE DIALOGUE IN SPANISH)

3. **Use 60 – 80 words to complete the dialogue between you and your friend from Peru, giving your responses.**

Your Peruvian friend has started a conversation with you online about sports. Complete the dialogue with him/her. Include:

(i) whether you play sports or not
(ii) your thoughts on the importance of sports
(iii) how often you exercise
(iv) popular sports and a sports personality in your country
(v) information about sports at your school

Responses to ALL the cues provided must be included in the completed dialogue.

Amigo/a: ¡Oye! Amigo/a.
Tú: ______________________________
Amigo/a Estoy muy bien, gracias. ¿Juegas los deportes?
Tú: ______________________________
Amigo/a: ¿Piensas que es importante jugar los deportes?
Tú: ______________________________
Amigo/a: ¿Por qué piensas así?
Tú: ______________________________
Amigo/a: ¿Y, cuántas veces a la semana ejerces?
Tú: ______________________________
Amigo/a: ¿Participas en la clase de educación física en tu colegio?
Tú: ______________________________
Amigo/a: ¿Cuáles son los deportes que haces en la clase de educación física?
Tú: ______________________________
Amigo/a: ¿Cuáles son los deportes más populares en tu país?
Tú: ______________________________
Amigo/a: ¿Quién es el/la deportista más famoso/a en tu país?
Tú: ______________________________
Amigo/a: ¿En qué deporte participa esta persona?
Tú: ______________________________
Amigo/a: ¿Hay un día de deportes en tu colegio?
Tú: ______________________________
Amigo/a: ¡Qué interesante! ¿Cuándo es normalmente?
Tú: ______________________________
Amigo/a: Bueno. Tengo que irme ahora. Nos vemos pronto.

Sección III Total = 20 Puntos

PARAGUAY
TERERÉ
HABAS DE SOJA
SALTOS DEL MONDAY

SECCIÓN IV

COMPRENSIÓN DE LECTURA (READING COMPREHENSION)
RESPONDE A CADA PREGUNTA (ANSWER ALL QUESTIONS)

4. **Lee la siguiente selección con cuidado y responde a las preguntas en INGLÉS.**

Read the following selection carefully. Do NOT translate but answer the questions in ENGLISH.

YOU WILL BE PENALIZED FOR DISREGARDING THESE INSTRUCTIONS.

Growing up in the Caribbean

Por muchos niños, jóvenes y adultos, la experiencia de crecer en el Caribe es realmente una experiencia única. Los niños y jóvenes pueden hacer muchas actividades para divertirse sin comprar cosas caras o aun gastar dinero. No es inusual ver a los jóvenes hacer y volar cometas en Turcos y Caicos. En Belice es normal para los chicos a trepar mangoteros para recoger la fruta o simplemente para esconder en un juego de escondite.

En Montserrat, jugar a las canicas* es una de las actividades de los niños. Las niñas prefieren jugar a la rayuela*. En cada país caribeño, es imposible viajar alrededor del país y no ver a los niños jugar un juego de fútbol en cualquier campo, incluso campos de caña de azúcar. Los jóvenes caribeños son tan creativos que usan papel para crear botas que ponen en el agua en la calle después de la lluvia para una carrera*. Estas actividades y más son las que nos conectamos.

(161 palabras)

***canicas – marbles**
***rayuela – hopscotch**
***carrera – race (competition)**

Answer the questions in ENGLISH, based on the selection above. Use a complete sentence for each response.

(a) For whom is the Caribbean experience unique? (3 puntos)

____

(b) What is said about money? (2 puntos)

____

(c) What is typical to see in Turks and Caicos? (2 puntos)

____

(d) Mention two (2) things children do in mango trees. (2 puntos)

____

(e) What is a preferred activity for boys in Montserrat? (2 puntos)

____

(f) How are girls in Montserrat different from boys? (2 puntos)

____

(g) Where in all Caribbean countries can boys be seen? (2 puntos)

____

(h) What do youngsters use to make boats? (1 punto)

____

(i) Why do Caribbean youngsters make these boats? (2 puntos)

____

(j) What is said about all these Caribbean activities? (2 puntos)

____

Sección IV Total = 20 Puntos

TOTAL PUNTOS POR PRUEBA = 100
FIN DE PRUEBA (END OF TEST)
REVISA TU TRABAJO POR FAVOR (PLEASE CHECK YOUR WORK)

PARAGUAY

TERERÉ

HABAS DE SOJA

SALTOS DEL MONDAY

PAPEL ADICIONAL/NO FALTA NADA DE ESTA PÁGINA

(EXTRA PAPER)/(NOTHING IS MISSING FROM THIS PAGE)

Grade 9

Term 2

PRACTICE TEST 2

PERÚ

ALFOMBRAS

LAS LLAMAS

MACHU PICCHU

No cometas los mismos errores

(Don't make the same mistakes)

Below are common mistakes made by students of Spanish. Please note the mistakes and the corrections given. By avoiding these mistakes, you will be sure to improve your writing skills in Spanish.

PUNTUACIÓN Y MAYÚSCULAS (PUNCTUATION AND CAPITALIZATION)		
Inglés	**Español con error**	**Español correcto**
1. Dear John, How are you?	Querido Juan, ¿Cómo estás?	Querido Juan: ¿Cómo estás?
2. It's very, very interesting.	Es muy, muy interesante.	Es muy muy interesante.
3. What did you do?	¿Qué hizo ud.?	¿Qué hizo Ud.?
4. February 14, 2026.	14 de Febrero de 2026.	14 de febrero de 2026.
5. Last night, I ate Italian food.	Anoche, yo comí la comida Italiana.	Anoche, yo comí la comida italiana.

LETRAS CON TILDES (LETTERS WITH TILDES)		
Inglés	**Español con error**	**Español correcto**
1. Yesterday, I studied history.	Ayer, yo estudie la historia.	Ayer, yo estudié la historia.
2. The little girl drank juice.	La ninita bebió jugo/zumo.	La niñita bebió jugo/zumo.
3. He bought my lunch.	Él compro mi almuerzo.	Él compró mi almuerzo.
4. I dreamt about the test.	Yo soné con la prueba.	Yo soñé con la prueba.
5. We played cricket.	Jugamos al beisbol.	Jugamos al béisbol.

EL VOCABULARIO (VOCABULARY)		
Inglés	**Español con error**	**Español correcto**
1. I sang at the party.	Yo canté en el partido.	Yo canté en la fiesta.
2. He wanted to assist the baby.	Él quiso asistir al bebé.	Él quiso ayudar al bebé.
3. I wrote a love letter.	Yo escribí una letra de amor.	Yo escribí una carta de amor.
4. You visited the college.	Tú visitaste el colegio.	Tú visitaste la universidad.
5. I disliked riding a horse.	No me gustó montar a cabello.	No me gustó montar a caballo.

Respuestas Abiertas (Free Response)

Nombre:______________________________ Apellido: ________________________

Clase:_______________________________ Profesor/a: ______________________

Fecha: ____

Duración: 90 minutos

INSTRUCCIONES

1. **Esta prueba tiene CUATRO (4) secciones. Responde a cada pregunta en este papel.**

   This test has FOUR (4) sections. Answer all questions on this paper.

2. **Sección I: Tiene DIEZ (10) situaciones. Responde a cada situación en ESPAÑOL.**

   Section I: Has TEN (10) situations. Respond to each in SPANISH.

3. **Sección II: Tiene una carta informal. Escribe la carta en ESPAÑOL.**

   Section II: Has an informal letter. Write the letter in SPANISH.

4. **Sección III: Tiene un diálogo. Rellena los espacios en ESPAÑOL.**

   Section III: Has a dialogue. Complete the dialogue in SPANISH.

5. **Sección IV: Tiene una comprensión de lectura. Responde a las DIEZ (10) preguntas en INGLÉS.**

   Section IV: Has a reading comprehension. Answer the TEN (10) questions in ENGLISH.

SECCIÓN I

LAS SITUACIONES ESCRITAS (WRITTEN SITUATIONS)
RESPONDE A CADA SITUACIÓN (RESPOND TO EACH SITUATION)

El año pasado mi familia fue a Méjico.

1. Write in SPANISH the information required by each of the situations given below. Do NOT write more than ONE sentence for each situation. For some situations, a complete sentence may not be necessary. Write each answer in the space provided.

(a) The Spanish embassy is doing a survey and sends you an email asking how often you study Spanish every week. What do you reply in your email?

(3 puntos)

____

(b) Your Cuban friend sends you a *WhatsApp* message asking if you watched the movie he/she recommended. What sentence do you text to reply?

(3 puntos)

____

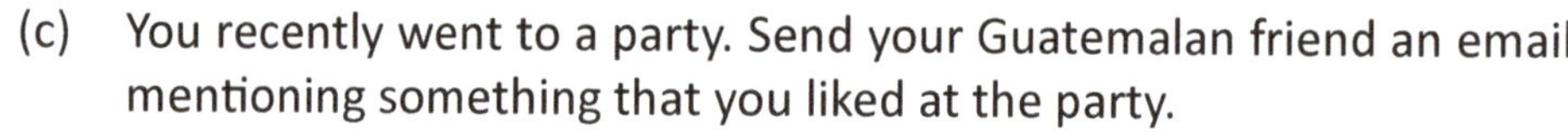

(c) You recently went to a party. Send your Guatemalan friend an email mentioning something that you liked at the party.

(3 puntos)

____

(d) One of your Spanish-speaking friends sends you a message asking you what you think of his/her new shoes. What do you reply?

(3 puntos)

____

(e) At an event at the Mexican embassy you receive a note from your crush asking you where you bought your shirt/blouse. What do you write in the note?

(3 puntos)

____

(f) Your Spanish teacher has asked students to write one thing they can do to live a healthy life. What do you write?

(3 puntos)

____

(g) You want to know what your Peruvian friend drank for breakfast. What do you ask him/her on *Instagram*?

(3 puntos)

____

(h) You see a post in Spanish on *Facebook* asking people if they prefer to play sports, musical instruments or games. Reply to the post stating your preference.

(3 puntos)

____

(i) It is the day after Labour Day and your Chilean friend sends you a message on *Twitter* asking you what you did for the environment. What do you reply?

(3 puntos)

____

(j) You and your friend went out yesterday. Send your Bolivian friend a message telling him/her something good that your friend did.

(3 puntos)

____

Sección I Total = 30 Puntos

PERÚ

ALFOMBRAS

LAS LLAMAS

MACHU PICCHU

SECCIÓN II

LA CARTA INFORMAL (INFORMAL LETTER)
ESCRIBE UNA CARTA EN ESPAÑOL (WRITE A LETTER IN SPANISH)

2. Using the following outline as a guide, write a letter in SPANISH of no more than 80 – 100 words.

YOU WILL BE PENALIZED FOR DISREGARDING THESE INSTRUCTIONS.

Yesterday, you represented your school at an event for third form students in your country and you did well. Write a letter to your Argentine pen pal in which you include:

(i) when you participated in the event and where
(ii) what activities you did
(iii) new friends you met and their schools
(iv) what you won for your school

(Do NOT write your real name and address, but include the date in Spanish and use the appropriate beginning and ending.)

Sección II Total = 30 Puntos

SECCIÓN III

EL DIÁLOGO CONTEXTUAL (CONTEXTUAL DIALOGUE)
LEE Y RELLENA EL DIÁLOGO EN ESPAÑOL
(READ AND COMPLETE THE DIALOGUE IN SPANISH)

PERÚ

3. Use 60 – 80 words to complete the dialogue between you and your Uruguayan friend on *WhatsApp*, giving your responses.

You received something special from a secret admirer and you are very excited. You start a conversation with your Uruguayan friend to tell him/her about it. Include:

(i) what the gift is
(ii) where you received the gift
(iii) what was written on the note accompanying the gift
(iv) what you are going to do with the gift
(v) how you feel about the gift

ALFOMBRAS

Responses to ALL the cues provided must be included in the completed dialogue.

Tú: **¡Hola! ¿Qué hay? Tengo buenas noticias.**
Uruguayo/a: ¡Epa! Estoy bien. ¿Qué noticias tienes?
Tú: ______________________________
Uruguayo/a: ¿De veras? ¿Qué recibiste?
Tú: ______________________________
Uruguayo/a: ¡Qué estúpendo! Descríbelo
Tú: ______________________________
Uruguago/a: ¿Y quién te mandó el regalo?
Tú: ______________________________
Uruguayo/a: ¿No sabes? ¿Piensas que es un/a estudiante de tu escuela?
Tú: ______________________________
Uruguayo/a: ¿Dónde recibiste el regalo?
Tú: ______________________________
Uruguayo/a: ¿Recibiste una nota con el regalo?
Tú: ______________________________
Uruguayo/a: ¿Qué escribió la persona en la nota?
Tú: ______________________________
Uruguayo/a: ¡Interesante! ¿Qué vas a hacer con el regalo?
Tú: ______________________________
Uruguayo/a: ¿Vas a decir a tus padres y parientes?
Tú: ______________________________
Uruguayo/a: ¿Por qué/no?
Tú: ______________________________
Uruguayo/a: ¿Cómo te sientes sobre el regalo?
Tú: ______________________________
Uruguayo/a: Genial. Aparentemente tienes un/a admirador/a secreto/a. Bueno, hasta luego.

LAS LLAMAS

MACHU PICCHU

Sección III Total = 20 Puntos

SECCIÓN IV

COMPRENSIÓN DE LECTURA (READING COMPREHENSION)
RESPONDE A CADA PREGUNTA (ANSWER ALL QUESTIONS)

4. **Lee la siguiente selección con cuidado y responde a las preguntas en INGLÉS.**

Read the following selection carefully. Do NOT translate but answer the questions in ENGLISH.

YOU WILL BE PENALIZED FOR DISREGARDING THESE INSTRUCTIONS..

Caribbean Quality: Support Our Own

Nadie puede negar que el Caribe está lleno de varios productos de alta calidad* que comparte con el mundo. En quizás cada país en la región hay distintos productos que son bien conocidos en el mundo. Cuba es conocida por el cigarro cubano. Las marcas* como 'Romeo y Julieta' y 'Cohiba' son famosas. El Café de las Montañas Azules es uno de los productos que Jamaica comparte con el mundo. Japón compra más de setenta porciento del café jamaicano.

El ron de la compañía 'Bacardi' en Puerto Rico que comenzó en el año 1862 es bien conocido por muchos. Además, podemos añadir el ron de 'El Dorado', una compañía guyanesa, a la lista. Barbados ofrece el algodón de 'Sea Island' que se describe como "el algodón más raro del mundo". El azúcar caribeño continua a ser muy importante hoy y Belice produce algunos de los mejores tipos de azúcar en la región. Debemos apoyarnos unos a otros para mejorar relaciones y economías regionales.

(161 palabras)

***calidad – quality**
***las marcas – brands**

Answer the questions in ENGLISH, based on the selection above. Use a complete sentence for each response.

(a) According to the passage, what can't people deny? **(3 puntos)**

____

____

(b) For what is Cuba known? **(1 punto)**

____

(c) Identify TWO (2) Cuban brands (2 puntos)

____

(d) What is said about Blue Mountain Coffee? (2 puntos)

____

(e) Describe the situation between Jamaica and Japan in the text. (2 puntos)

____

(f) Where is the 'Bacardi' company and when was it started? (2 puntos)

____

(g) Identify another rum brand mentioned and its country (2 puntos)

____

(h) How is the Barbadian product described? (2 puntos)

____

(i) What is said about Caribbean sugar? (2 puntos)

____

(j) Why should Caribbean countries support each other? (2 puntos)

____

Sección IV Total = 20 Puntos

TOTAL PUNTOS POR PRUEBA = 100
FIN DE PRUEBA (END OF TEST)
REVISA TU TRABAJO POR FAVOR (PLEASE CHECK YOUR WORK)

PERÚ

ALFOMBRAS

LAS LLAMAS

MACHU PICCHU

Las marcas populares

- El café de las Montañas Azules
- Cohiba
- Bacardi
- Azúcar de Belice
- El Dorado
- Sea Island Cotton

Productos de alta calidad.

PAPEL ADICIONAL/NO FALTA NADA DE ESTA PÁGINA

(EXTRA PAPER)/(NOTHING IS MISSING FROM THIS PAGE)

Grade 9
Term 3
PRACTICE TEST 1

GUATEMALA
(LAND OF MANY TREES)
QUETZAL

LA ALPACA

TIKAL

No cometas los mismos errores

(Don't make the same mistakes)

Below are common mistakes made by students of Spanish. Please note the mistakes and the corrections given. By avoiding these mistakes, you will be sure to improve your writing skills in Spanish.

LA GRAMÁTICA (GRAMMAR)		
Inglés	**Español con error**	**Español correcto**
1. I went to the mall.	Yo fue al centro comercial.	Yo fui al centro comercial.
2. I wanted to swim in the sea.	Yo quiero nadar en el mar.	Yo quise nadar en el mar.
3. I want to invite Rihanna.	Yo quiero invitar Rihanna.	Yo quiero invitar a Rihanna.
4. I hope to travel to Africa.	Yo espero viajo a África.	Yo espero viajar a África.
5. I had to stay home.	Yo tuve que quedarse en casa.	Yo tuve que quedarme en casa.

LA ORTOGRAFÍA (SPELLING)		
Inglés	**Español con error**	**Español correcto**
1. We went to the market.	Nosotros fuemos al mercado.	Nosotros fuimos al mercado.
2. I arrived late.	Yo llegé tarde.	Yo llegué tarde.
3. We took photos of the flowers.	Sacamos photos de las flores.	Sacamos fotos de las flores.
4. We won a gold medal.	Ganamos una medala de oro.	Ganamos una medalla de oro.
5. I hope to buy a cellular phone.	Yo espero comprar un teléfono cellular.	Yo espero comprar un teléfono celular.

EL ORDEN DE LAS PALABRAS (WORD ORDER)		
Inglés	**Español con error**	**Español correcto**
1. Three days ago, I drank milk.	Tres días hace, yo bebí leche.	Hace tres días, yo bebí leche.
2. I saw some cheap shirts.	Vi unas baratas camisas.	Vi unas camisas baratas.
3. Why didn't you study?	¿Por qué tú no estudiaste?	¿Por qué no estudiaste tú?
4. I went to a small, vegetable market.	Fui a un pequeño, verduras mercado.	Fui a un mercado de verduras pequeño.

Respuestas Abiertas (Free Response)

Nombre:_____________________________ Apellido: ________________________

Clase:________________________________ Profesor/a: ______________________

Fecha: ____

Duración: 90 minutos

INSTRUCCIONES

1. **Esta prueba tiene CUATRO (4) secciones. Responde a cada pregunta en este papel.**

   This test has FOUR (4) sections. Answer all questions on this paper.

2. **Sección I: Tiene DIEZ (10) situaciones. Responde a cada situación en ESPAÑOL.**

   Section I: Has TEN (10) situations. Respond to each in SPANISH.

3. **Sección II: Tiene una carta informal. Escribe la carta en ESPAÑOL.**

   Section II: Has an informal letter. Write the letter in SPANISH.

4. **Sección III: Tiene un diálogo. Rellena los espacios en ESPAÑOL.**

   Section III: Has a dialogue. Complete the dialogue in SPANISH.

5. **Sección IV: Tiene una comprensión de lectura. Responde a las DIEZ (10) preguntas en INGLÉS.**

   Section IV: Has a reading comprehension. Answer the TEN (10) questions in ENGLISH.

SECCIÓN I

LAS SITUACIONES ESCRITAS (WRITTEN SITUATIONS)
RESPONDE A CADA SITUACIÓN (RESPOND TO EACH SITUATION)

1. Write in SPANISH the information required by each of the situations given below. Do NOT write more than ONE sentence for each situation. For some situations, a complete sentence may not be necessary. Write each answer in the space provided.

(a) You are just returning from the market. Send your Costa Rican friend a message telling him/her what you did there.

(3 puntos)

___

(b) Your Peruvian cousin wants to know something about a shopping mall in your country. What information do you provide in the email you send him/her?

(3 puntos)

___

(c) There is an exchange student in your class who speaks Spanish. You want to know what he/she did last night. What do you ask in the note you send him/her?

(3 puntos)

___

(d) You did not go to school yesterday and you received a message from your Spanish teacher asking you where you went. What do you reply in your message?

(3 puntos)

___

(e) You went on a trip and did not do what you wanted to and are disappointed. Send your Venezuelan friend a message online telling him/her what you wanted to do.

(3 puntos)

___

(f) You found something in your class and a classmate asked in the Spanish *WhatsApp* group where you put it. Reply to the message by mentioning the item.

(3 puntos)

____

(g) Your Honduran friend has asked you what he/she can buy for his/her mother's birthday. What advice do you give him/her?

(3 puntos)

____

(h) You went to a Spanish supermarket but when you reached home you realised you did not receive an item. Send a message on the website explaining this.

(3 puntos)

____

(i) You were recently awarded top student in your class and your Spanish teacher asked you to write what you had to do to win the award. What do you write?

(3 puntos)

____

(j) Your Mexican friend sent you a picture of something he/she bought. You want to know how much he/she paid for it. What do you ask in the message you send?

(3 puntos)

____

Sección I Total = 30 Puntos

SECCIÓN II

LA CARTA INFORMAL (INFORMAL LETTER)
ESCRIBE UNA CARTA EN ESPAÑOL (WRITE A LETTER IN SPANISH)

2. **Using the following outline as a guide, write a letter in SPANISH of no more than 80 – 100 words.**

YOU WILL BE PENALIZED FOR DISREGARDING THESE INSTRUCTIONS.

You and your family recently spent a day at the shopping mall. Write a letter to your Ecuadorian pen pal telling him/her about it. Be sure to include:

(i) when, where and with whom you went
(ii) how you got to the mall
(iii) what activities you did there
(iv) what you ate and drank

(Do NOT write your real name and address, but include the date in Spanish and use the appropriate beginning and ending.)

Sección II Total = 30 Puntos

SECCIÓN III

EL DIÁLOGO CONTEXTUAL (CONTEXTUAL DIALOGUE)
LEE Y RELLENA EL DIÁLOGO EN ESPAÑOL
(READ AND COMPLETE THE DIALOGUE IN SPANISH)

3. Use 60 – 80 words to complete the dialogue between you and your Latin American friend on *Messenger*, giving your responses.

You have to make a presentation in Spanish in front of your school and you are nervous. You have a conversation online with your Spanish-speaking friend. Include:

(i) when and where you have the presentation
(ii) reason for the presentation
(iii) what your classmates will do
(iv) how you feel about the topic
(v) advice your Spanish teacher gave you

Responses to ALL the cues provided must be included in the completed dialogue.

Tú: **¡Hola! Necesito tu ayuda.**
Amigo/a: ¡Hola! ¿Cuál es tu problema?
Tú: ______________________
Amigo/a: ¿Presentación? ¿Cuándo?
Tú: ______________________
Amigo/a: ¿Y cuál es el tema de la presentación?
Tú: ______________________
Amigo/a: Bueno. Es muy fácil. ¿Dónde vas a hacer la presentación?
Tú: ______________________
Amigo/a: Pues, ¿quiénes van a estar allí para la presentación?
Tú: ______________________
Amigo/a: ¿Por qué tienes que hacer esta presentación?
Tú: ______________________
Amigo/a: ¡Estupendo! ¿A qué hora del día es esta presentación?
Tú: ______________________
Amigo/a: ¿Y qué van a hacer los otros estudiantes en tu clase?
Tú: ______________________
Amigo/a: Vale. ¿Te gusta este tema?
Tú: ______________________
Amigo/a: ¿Por qué no?
Tú: ______________________
Amigo/a: ¡Qué lástima! ¿Cuándo vas a escribir la presentación?
Tú: ______________________
Amigo/a: Genial. ¿Qué dijo tu profesor/a de español sobre la presentación?
Tú: ______________________
____
Amigo/a: Bueno. Buena suerte. ¡Puedes hacerlo!

Sección III Total = 20 Puntos

SECCIÓN IV

COMPRENSIÓN DE LECTURA (READING COMPREHENSION)
RESPONDE A CADA PREGUNTA (ANSWER ALL QUESTIONS)

4. Lee la siguiente selección con cuidado y responde a las preguntas en INGLÉS.

Read the following selection carefully. Do NOT translate but answer the questions in ENGLISH.

YOU WILL BE PENALIZED FOR DISREGARDING THESE INSTRUCTIONS.

Botanic Gardens of St. Vincent and the Grenadines

Situado en Kingstown, la capital de San Vicente y las Granadinas, está el famoso Jardín Botánico. Este jardín maravilloso es el jardín botánico más viejo en el hemisferio occidental. En 1765, un hombre, el General Robert Melville se fundó el jardín y ahora hay muchas especies de plantas y animales, como pájaros y lagartos*. La gente de San Vicente y las Granadinas es muy orgullosa de su jardín que tiene más de doscientos cincuenta años.

En el jardín, puedes ver el 'árbol de *soufriere*' que es la flor nacional del país. También, hay árboles como: la fruta del pan (que primero, el Capitán William Bligh trajo allí), el mango y por supuesto, la palma y el coco. El ave nacional, el loro de San Vicente, está en el jardín también. La historia del Jardín Botánico es muy única e importante a los de San Vicente y las Granadinas.

(148 palabras)

***los lagartos – lizards**

Answer the questions in ENGLISH, based on the selection above. Use a complete sentence for each response.

(a) What is the capital of Saint Vincent and the Grenadines? **(1 punto)**

____

(b) How does the garden compare to others in the Western hemisphere? **(2 puntos)**

____

(c) Who founded the garden and when was it founded? **(2 puntos)**

____

(d) What is said about species? **(2 puntos)**

____

(e) How do Saint Vincentians feel about the garden? **(1 punto)**

____

(f) What is *'soufriere'*? **(2 puntos)**

____

(g) What is said about Captain William Bligh? **(3 puntos)**

____

(h) List THREE (3) types of trees in the garden. **(3 puntos)**

____

(i) What is said about parrot? **(2 puntos)**

____

(j) Describe the history of the Botanic Gardens. **(2 puntos)**

____

Sección IV Total = 20 Puntos

TOTAL PUNTOS POR PRUEBA = 100
FIN DE PRUEBA (END OF TEST)
REVISA TU TRABAJO POR FAVOR (PLEASE CHECK YOUR WORK)

PAPEL ADICIONAL/NO FALTA NADA DE ESTA PÁGINA

(EXTRA PAPER)/(NOTHING IS MISSING FROM THIS PAGE)

Grade 9

Term 3

PRACTICE TEST 2

URUGUAY

EL JAGUAR (JAGUAR)

GAUCHO

LA CATEDRAL METROPOLITANA DE MONTEVIDEO

No cometas los mismos errores

(Don't make the same mistakes)

Below are common mistakes made by students of Spanish. Please note the mistakes and the corrections given. By avoiding these mistakes, you will be sure to improve your writing skills in Spanish.

PUNTUACIÓN Y MAYÚSCULAS (PUNCTUATION AND CAPITALIZATION)		
Inglés	**Español con error**	**Español correcto**
1. Hahaha	Jajaja	Ja, ja, ja.
2. I bought the shirt for $1,200.00	Yo compré la camisa por $1,200.00	Yo compré la camisa por 1.200,00 $
3. She had some DVDs.	Ella tuvo unos DVDs.	Ella tuvo unos DVD.
4. We had to speak Spanish.	Tuvimos que hablar Español.	Tuvimos que hablar español.
5. In August, I went to the beach.	En Agosto, yo fui a la playa.	En agosto, yo fui a la playa.

LETRAS CON TILDES (LETTERS WITH TILDES)		
Inglés	**Español con error**	**Español correcto**
1. Yesterday, I went to a concert.	Ayer, yo fuí a un concierto.	Ayer, yo fui a un concierto.
2. The cat is the size of the dog.	El gato es el tamano del perro.	El gato es el tamaño del perro.
3. I saw the event on TV.	Yo vío el evento en la televisión.	Yo vi el evento en la televisión.
4. My classmates are going to present also.	Mis companeros de clase van a presentar también.	Mis compañeros de clase van a presentar también.
5. There is a celebration.	Hay una celebracion.	Hay una celebración.

EL VOCABULARIO (VOCABULARY)		
Inglés	**Español con error**	**Español correcto**
1. It cost 200 dollars.	Costó 200 dolores.	Costó 200 dólares.
2. The food is very expensive.	La comida es muy carro.	La comida es muy cara.
3. I did no buy ice cream, but I bought cake.	Yo no compré helado, pero compré el pastel.	Yo no compré helado, sino compré el pastel.
4. Water is better than juice.	El agua es mayor que el jugo.	El agua es mejor que el jugo.
5. I spent a lot of money.	Yo gasté mucho dólar.	Yo gasté mucho dinero.

Respuestas Abiertas (Free Response)

Nombre:________________________ Apellido: ____________________

Clase:________________________ Profesor/a: ____________________

Fecha: ____

Duración: 90 minutos

INSTRUCCIONES

1. **Esta prueba tiene CUATRO (4) secciones. Responde a cada pregunta en este papel.**

   This test has FOUR (4) sections. Answer all questions on this paper.

2. **Sección I: Tiene DIEZ (10) situaciones. Responde a cada situación en ESPAÑOL.**

   Section I: Has TEN (10) situations. Respond to each in SPANISH.

3. **Sección II: Tiene una carta informal. Escribe la carta en ESPAÑOL.**

   Section II: Has an informal letter. Write the letter in SPANISH.

4. **Sección III: Tiene un diálogo. Rellena los espacios en ESPAÑOL.**

   Section III: Has a dialogue. Complete the dialogue in SPANISH.

5. **Sección IV: Tiene una comprensión de lectura. Responde a las DIEZ (10) preguntas en INGLÉS.**

   Section IV: Has a reading comprehension. Answer the TEN (10) questions in ENGLISH.

Equatorial Guinea

La República
de Guinea
Ecuatorial

- Cacao
- Elefantes
- Petróleo
- Malamba

SECCIÓN I

LAS SITUACIONES ESCRITAS (WRITTEN SITUATIONS)
RESPONDE A CADA SITUACIÓN (RESPOND TO EACH SITUATION)

1. **Write in SPANISH the information required by each of the situations given below. Do NOT write more than ONE sentence for each situation. For some situations, a complete sentence may not be necessary. Write each answer in the space provided.**

(a) Your classmate bought an item of jewellery and your Spanish friend sent you a message asking what your classmate bought. What do you reply?

(3 puntos)

____

(b) You were late for school this morning. What reason do you give in the message you write to your Spanish teacher?

(3 puntos)

____

(c) A Spanish speaker came to your school to make a presentation. Write one thing that you liked about the presentation on the feedback form.

(3 puntos)

____

(d) Your Nicaraguan friend sends you a message online asking you how many hours you spend on a weekend surfing the internet. What do you reply?

(3 puntos)

____

(e) You receive a message in Spanish from your friend asking you whether you think water is better than juice. What do you reply?

(3 puntos)

____

(f) You want to know when your friend did something specific. What do you ask in the message you send on *Instagram*?

(3 puntos)

____

(g) Your school festival is coming up. Send your Paraguayan friend a message indicating who you want to invite to the festival and why.

(3 puntos)

____

(h) Your Cuban friend sends you a picture of his/her collection of key rings from around the world and asks what you collect. What do you reply in your message?

(3 puntos)

____

(i) It is the end of the school year and your Spanish teacher asks each student to write one thing they enjoyed during the school year. What do you write?

(3 puntos)

____

(j) Your Mexican friend has an exam and sends you a message saying that he/she did not study. What do you ask in the message you send him/her online?

(3 puntos)

____

Sección I Total = 30 Puntos

URUGUAY

JAGUAR

GAUCHO

MONTEVIDEO CATHEDRAL

SECCIÓN II

LA CARTA INFORMAL (INFORMAL LETTER)
ESCRIBE UNA CARTA EN ESPAÑOL (WRITE A LETTER IN SPANISH)

2. **Using the following outline as a guide, write a letter in SPANISH of no more than 80 – 100 words.**

YOU WILL BE PENALIZED FOR DISREGARDING THESE INSTRUCTIONS.

Your country won an event and everyone is happy. Write a letter to your friend from Chile about it. Be sure to include:

(i) what the event was and when your country won it
(ii) where you saw the results of the event
(iii) how you feel about the victory
(iv) how people are celebrating

____

____

____

____

____

____

____

____

____

____

____

____

____

____

(Do NOT write your real name and address, but include the date in Spanish and use the appropriate beginning and ending.)

Sección II Total = 30 Puntos

SECCIÓN III

EL DIÁLOGO CONTEXTUAL (CONTEXTUAL DIALOGUE)
LEE Y RELLENA EL DIÁLOGO EN ESPAÑOL
(READ AND COMPLETE THE DIALOGUE IN SPANISH)

URUGUAY

3. Use 60 – 80 words to complete the dialogue between you and your Colombian friend on *Twitter* giving your responses.

A new restaurant has opened in your country and you and your friends decide to go. Complete this dialogue you have with your Colombian friend online while you are there. Include:

(i) what type of food the restaurant sells
(ii) the types of desserts on the menu
(iii) what you are going to order
(iv) a description of the ambience in the restaurant
(v) what your friends are going to order

JAGUAR

Responses to ALL the cues provided must be included in the completed dialogue.

Colombiano/a: ¡Hola! ¿Qué tal y dónde estás?
Tú: ____________________
Colombiano/a: ¿De veras? ¿Cuál restaurante?
Tú: ____________________
Colombiano/a: ¿Y qué tipo de comida sirven allí?
Tú: ____________________
Colombiano/a: Bueno. Dime, ¿con quién estás allí?
Tú: ____________________
Colombiano/a: ¿Amigos? Te envidio* ¿Cuáles son los postres que tienen? (Envidiar – to envy)
Tú: ____________________
____
Colombiano/a: ¡Ay! Me gustan los postres. ¿Tienen un plato del día?
Tú: ____________________
Colombiano/a: ¿Qué vas a ordenar?
Tú: ____________________
Colombiano/a: ¡Es delicioso! ¿Cuánto es?
Tú: ____________________
Colombiano/a: Vale. No es tan caro. ¿Qué bebidas hay en el menú?
Tú: ____________________
Colombiano/a: ¿Y cuál vas a tomar?
Tú: ____________________
Colombiano/a: Describe la atmósfera del restaurante.
Tú: ____________________
Colombiano/a: ¡Perfecto! ¿Qué van a tomar tus amigos?
Tú: ____________________
Colombiano/a: Bueno. Buen provecho. Quiero ir a este restaurante contigo cuando visite.

GAUCHO

MONTEVIDEO CATHEDRAL

Sección III Total = 20 Puntos

SECCIÓN IV

COMPRENSIÓN DE LECTURA (READING COMPREHENSION)
RESPONDE A CADA PREGUNTA (ANSWER ALL QUESTIONS)

4. **Lee la siguiente selección con cuidado y responde a las preguntas en INGLÉS.**

Read the following selection carefully. Do NOT translate but answer the questions in ENGLISH.

YOU WILL BE PENALIZED FOR DISREGARDING THESE INSTRUCTIONS.

<u>Derek Walcott: A Caribbean Giant</u>

Derek Walcott era un poeta de Santa Lucía. Walcott nació en Castries en el año 1930 y murió recientemente en 2017. En el año 1992, Walcott recibió el Premio Nobel por la literatura. Walcott se puso* la segunda persona del Caribe que recibió este premio internacional. Como joven, Walcott recibió entrenamiento como pintor. Además, Walcott asistió a la Universidad de las Antillas en Jamaica. Él estudió la literatura inglesa, francés y latín.

Por más de dos décadas, Walcott era profesor universitario en la Universidad de Boston en los Estados Unidos. La religión, el arte, la historia del Caribe y el paisaje son temas comunes en los poemas de Walcott. Hoy en día, muchos estudiantes en la región estudian la poesía de Walcott, como, *Another Life (Otra vida), Star-Apple Kingdom* y su obra* popular, *Ti-Jean y sus hermanos.* Walcott es una inspiración para todas las personas de la comunidad caribeña.

(150 palabras)

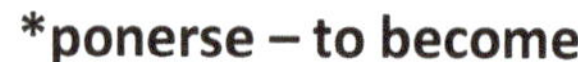

***ponerse – to become**
*** obra – play (work)**

Answer the questions in ENGLISH, based on the selection above. Use a complete sentence for each response.

(a) What was the nationality of Derek Walcott? **(1 punto)**

____

(b) At what age did Walcott die? **(1 punto)**

____

(c) What major award did he win and for what area? (2 puntos)

____

(d) In what field/area did Walcott receive training? (2 puntos)

____

(e) Walcott was a student at which university? (2 puntos)

____

(f) What did he study at university? (3 puntos)

____

(g) For how long was he a professor at Boston University? (2 puntos)

____

(h) List THREE (3) common themes in Walcott's work. (3 puntos)

____

(i) What is said about *Ti-Jean and His Brothers*? (2 puntos)

____

(j) To whom is Walcott an inspiration? (2 puntos)

____

Sección IV Total = 20 Puntos

TOTAL PUNTOS POR PRUEBA = 100
FIN DE PRUEBA (END OF TEST)
REVISA TU TRABAJO POR FAVOR (PLEASE CHECK YOUR WORK)

URUGUAY

JAGUAR

GAUCHO

MONTEVIDEO CATHEDRAL

PAPEL ADICIONAL/NO FALTA NADA DE ESTA PÁGINA

(EXTRA PAPER)/(NOTHING IS MISSING FROM THIS PAGE)

Lista De Verbos Útiles

LOS VERBOS - AR

ESPAÑOL	INGLÉS	ESPAÑOL	INGLÉS
ACEPTAR	TO ACCEPT	INVITAR	TO INVITE
ACOMPAÑAR	TO ACCOMPANY	JUNTAR	TO JOIN
ADMIRAR	TO ADMIRE	LAMENTAR	TO BE SORRY ABOUT
AGREGAR	TO ADD	LAVAR	TO WASH
AHORRAR	TO SAVE (MONEY)	LIMPIAR	TO CLEAN
ANDAR	TO WALK	LLEGAR	TO ARRIVE
APAGAR	TO TURN OFF	LLENAR	TO FILL
AYUDAR	TO HELP	LLEVAR	TO WEAR; TO CARRY
BAILAR	TO DANCE	LLORAR	TO CRY
BESAR	TO KISS	LUCHAR	TO FIGHT
BORRAR	TO ERASE	MANDAR	TO SEND
BUSCAR	TO SEEK; TO SEARCH	MANEJAR	TO DRIVE
CALZAR	TO WEAR (SHOES)	MARCAR UN GOL	TO SCORE A GOAL
CAMBIAR	TO CHANGE	MEJORAR	TO BETTER; IMPROVE
CAMINAR	TO WALK	MIRAR	TO WATCH; LOOK (AT)
CANTAR	TO SING	MONTAR	TO RIDE
CASTIGAR	TO PUNISH	NADAR	TO SWIM
CELEBRAR	TO CELEBRATE	NAVEGAR	TO BROWSE (NET)
CENAR	TO EAT DINNER	NECESITAR	TO NEED
CHARLAR	TO CHAT	NEGAR	TO DENY
COCINAR	TO COOK	ORDENAR	TO ORDER
COLECCIONAR	TO COLLECT	PAGAR	TO PAY (FOR)

ESPAÑOL	INGLÉS	ESPAÑOL	INGLÉS
COMPRAR	TO BUY	GOZAR (DE)	TO ENJOY
CONTESTAR	TO ANSWER	GRITAR	TO SHOUT
CONTINUAR	TO CONTINUE	HABLAR	TO SPEAK; TO TALK
CORTAR	TO CUT	HALLAR	TO FIND
CREAR	TO CREATE	HORNEAR	TO BAKE
CUIDAR	TO CARE (FOR)	PARAR	TO STOP
CULTIVAR	TO CULTIVATE	PASAR	TO PASS;
DAÑAR	TO DESTROY	SPEND TIME	PATEAR
DESAYUNAR	TO EAT BREAKFAST	TO KICK	PATINAR
DESCANSAR	TO REST	TO SKATE	PESCAR
DESEAR	TO WANT; TO WISH	TO FISH PINTAR	TO PAINT
DISEÑAR	TO DESIGN	PLANCHAR	TO IRON
DOBLAR	TO TURN	PLANTAR	TO PLANT
DURAR	TO LAST (TIME)	PRACTICAR	TO PRACTICE
EMPUJAR	TO PUSH	PREGUNTAR	TO ASK
ENSEÑAR	TO TEACH	PRESTAR	TO LEND
ENTRAR	TO ENTER	PRONUNCIAR	TO PRONOUNCE
ENVIDIAR	TO ENVY	QUEMAR	TO BURN
ESCUCHAR	TO LISTEN	REGRESAR	TO RETURN
ESPERAR	TO HOPE; TO WAIT	REPARAR	TO REPAIR; TO FIX
ESTUDIAR	TO STUDY	REPRESENTAR	TO REPRESENT
EXPERIMENTAR	TO EXPERIENCE	ROBAR	TO ROB; TO STEAL
FUNCIONAR	TO FUNCTION; TO OPERATE	SACAR	TO TAKE (OUT/PHOTO)
GANAR	TO WIN; TO EARN	SALTAR	TO JUMP
GASTAR	TO SPEND (MONEY)	SALUDAR	TO GREET

ESPAÑOL	INGLÉS	ESPAÑOL	INGLÉS
SELECCIONAR	TO SELECT	TRATAR DE	TO TRY (TO)
TERMINAR	TO END	TREPAR	TO CLIMB
TOCAR	TO TOUCH; TO PLAY AN INSTRUMENT	USAR	TO USE
TOMAR	TO TAKE; EAT; DRINK	VIAJAR	TO TRAVEL
TRABAJAR	TO WORK	VISITAR	TO VISIT

LOS VERBOS – ER & IR

LOS VERBOS – ER		LOS VERBOS – IR	
ESPAÑOL	**INGLÉS**	**ESPAÑOL**	**INGLÉS**
APRENDER	TO LEARN	ABRIR	TO OPEN
BARRER	TO SWEEP	AÑADIR	TO ADD
BEBER	TO DRINK	APLAUDIR	TO APPLAUD
COMER	TO EAT	ASISTIR A	TO ATTEND
COMPRENDER	TO UNDERSTAND	COMPARTIR	TO SHARE
CORRER	TO RUN	CUBRIR	TO COVER
CREER	TO BELIEVE	DECIDIR	TO DECIDE
DEBER	TO MUST; OUGHT TO	DESCRIBIR	TO DESCRIBE
ESCONDER	TO HIDE SOMETHING	DIVIDIR	TO DIVIDE
LEER	TO READ	ESCRIBIR	TO WRITE
PROMETER	TO PROMISE	ESCRIBIR A MÁQUINA	TO TYPE
RESPONDER	TO ANSWER	PARTIR	TO LEAVE; DEPART
ROMPER	TO BREAK	PERMITIR	TO ALLOW
TEMER	TO FEAR; BE AFRAID	RECIBIR	TO RECEIVE; GET
TOSER	TO COUGH	SUBIR	TO CLIMB; GO UP
VENDER	TO SELL	VIVIR	TO LIVE

El Tiempo Presente De Indicativo

VERBOS IRREGULARES

LOS VERBOS – U-UE & E-I

LOS VERBOS – U-UE (Tiempo Presente)		LOS VERBOS – E-I (Tiempo Presente)	
ESPAÑOL	INGLÉS	ESPAÑOL	INGLÉS
JUGAR	TO PLAY (SPORT/GAME)	DESPEDIRSE (DE)*	TO TAKE LEAVE; TO SAY GOODBYE
		PEDIR	TO ASK FOR; TO ORDER
		REÍR (SE)	TO LAUGH
		REPETIR	TO REPEAT
		SEGUIR	TO FOLLOW; TO CONTINUE
		SERVIR	TO SERVE
		SONREÍR (SE)	TO SMILE
		VESTIRSE*	TO GET DRESSED

LOS VERBOS – O-UE & E-IE

LOS VERBOS – O-UE (Tiempo Presente)		LOS VERBOS – E-IE (Tiempo Presente)	
ESPAÑOL	INGLÉS	ESPAÑOL	INGLÉS
ACOSTARSE*	TO GO TO BED	ATRAVESAR	TO CROSS
ALMORZAR	TO EAT LUNCH	CERRAR	TO CLOSE
CONTAR	TO COUNT	COMENZAR	TO BEGIN
COSTAR	TO COST	DESPERTARSE*	TO WAKE UP; AWAKE

LOS VERBOS – O-UE (Tiempo Presente)		LOS VERBOS – E-IE (Tiempo Presente)	
ESPAÑOL	**INGLÉS**	**ESPAÑOL**	**INGLÉS**
DORMIR	TO SLEEP	DIVERTIRSE*	TO ENJOY ONESELF
DORMIRSE*	TO FALL ASLEEP	EMPEZAR	TO BEGIN
ENCONTRAR	TO MEET; TO FIND	ENCENDER	TO LIGHT; SWITCH ON
LLOVER	TO RAIN	ENTENDER	TO UNDERSTAND
MOSTRAR	TO SHOW	NEVAR	TO SNOW
PODER	TO CAN; TO BE ABLE	PENSAR	TO THINK
RECORDAR	TO REMEMBER	PERDER	TO LOSE
SONAR	TO SOUND; TO RING	PREFERIR	TO PREFER
SOÑAR CON	TO DREAM (ABOUT)	QUERER	TO LOVE; TO WANT
VOLAR	TO FLY	SENTARSE*	TO SIT DOWN
VOLVER	TO RETURN (A PLACE)	SENTIR	TO FEEL; TO BE SORRY

VERBOS EN LA TERCERA PERSONA

These verbs are often used in the third person.

ESPAÑOL	INGLÉS	ESPAÑOL	INGLÉS
DOLER	TO BE PAINFUL	ENCANTAR	TO LIKE; DELIGHT
GUSTAR	TO LIKE	IMPORTAR	TO MATTER
INTERESAR	TO BE INTERESTED		

LOS VERBOS REFLEXIVOS

ESPAÑOL	INGLÉS	ESPAÑOL	INGLÉS
AFEITARSE	TO SHAVE	ALEGRARSE	TO BE GLAD

LOS VERBOS REFLEXIVOS (cont'd.)			
ESPAÑOL	**INGLÉS**	**ESPAÑOL**	**INGLÉS**
ASUSTARSE	TO BE FRIGHTENED	BAÑARSE	TO BATHE
CALLARSE	TO KEEP QUIET(STILL)	CEPILLARSE	TO BRUSH (TEETH, HAIR)
DUCHARSE	TO SHOWER	EMOCIONARSE	TO GET EXCITED
ENOJARSE	TO GET ANGRY	EQUIVOCARSE	TO BE MISTAKEN
LEVANTARSE	TO GET UP	LLAMARSE	TO BE CALLED (NAMED)
MAQUILLARSE	TO PUT ON MAKEUP	PEINARSE	TO COMB ONE'S HAIR
QUEDARSE	TO STAY; TO REMAIN	QUEJARSE	TO COMPLAIN
QUITARSE	TO TAKE OFF (CLOTHES)	SECARSE	TO DRY (ONESELF)
SORPRENDERSE	TO BE SURPRISED		

Verbos Irregulares

VERBOS – CER Y CIR & GER Y GIR

VERBOS – CER Y CIR		VERBOS – GER Y GIR	
ESPAÑOL	**INGLÉS**	**ESPAÑOL**	**INGLÉS**
CRECER	TO GROW	COGER	TO CATCH
CONOCER	TO KNOW SOMEONE; MEET	CORREGIR	TO CORRECT
EJERCER	TO EXERCISE	ESCOGER	TO CHOOSE
INTRODUCIR	TO INTRODUCE	PROTEGER	TO PROTECT
NACER	TO BE BORN	RECOGER	TO PICK; GATHER
OFRECER	TO OFFER		
TRADUCIR	TO TRANSLATE		
PARECER	TO SEEM; TO APPEAR TO BE		

OTROS VERBOS IRREGULARES

ESPAÑOL	INGLÉS	ESPAÑOL	INGLÉS
CAER	TO FALL	DAR	TO GIVE
DECIR	TO SAY; TO TELL	ESTAR	TO BE
HACER	TO DO; TO MAKE	HACERSE	TO BECOME
IR	TO GO	OÍR	TO HEAR
PONER	TO PUT	SABER	TO KNOW (SOMETHING)
SALIR	TO LEAVE SOMEWHERE	SER	TO BE
TENER	TO HAVE	TRAER	TO BRING
VENIR	TO COME	VER	TO SEE

EXPRESIONES CON VERBOS

ESPAÑOL	INGLÉS	ESPAÑOL	INGLÉS
ESTAR LISTO/A	TO BE READY	ESTAR POR	TO BE IN FAVOUR OF
ESTAR SEGURO/A	TO BE SURE	PONER LA MESA	TO SET THE TABLE
SER LISTO/A	TO BE SMART	TENER CALOR	TO BE HOT
TENER CUIDADO	TO BE CAREFUL	TENER ÉXITO	TO BE SUCCESSFUL
TENER FRÍO	TO BE COLD	TENER HAMBRE	TO BE HUNGRY

Lista De Adjetivos

CON GÉNEROS NEUTROS

(List of neuter gender adjectives)

Categorías	Español	Inglés
1. La personalidad	1. Leal / Fiel 2. Humilde 3. Paciente 4. Elegante 5. Amable 6. Inteligente 7. Cortés 8. Desagradable 9. Responsable 10. Valiente 11. Diligente	1. Loyal / Faithful 2. Humble 3. Patient 4. Elegant 5. Friendly, nice, polite 6. Intelligent 7. Courteous, polite 8. Unpleasant 9. Responsible 10. Brave 11. Hardworking / Diligent
2. El color	12. Verde 13. Azul 14. Gris 15. Púrpura	12. Green 13. Blue 14. Grey 15. Purple
3. Físico	16. Grande 17. Joven 18. Fuerte 19. Débil	16. Big, Large, Tall 17. Young 18. Strong 19. Weak
4. La cosa	20. Importante 21. Imposible 22. Excelente 23. Fácil 24. Difícil 25. Interesante 26. Dulce 27. Emocionante 28. Esencial	20. Important 21. Impossible 22. Excellent 23. Easy 24. Difficult 25. Interesting 26. Sweet 27. Exciting 28. Essential
5. La emoción	29. Feliz 30. Triste*	29. Happy 30. Sad

Nota bien:
***Triste – usa el verbo ESTAR (Uses the verb ESTAR).**

IDIOMÁTICAS ÚTILES

GRADE 7

ESPAÑOL	INGLÉS	ESPAÑOL	INGLÉS
1. Tener (número) año.	To be (number) years old.	Tengo doce años.	I am twelve years old.
2. Hace (tiempo)	It is (weather condition)	Hace sol. Hace viento.	It is sunny It is windy.
3. En punto	On the dot / sharp (time)	A las tres en punto.	At three o'clock sharp.
4. A eso de	At or about	A eso de las dos.	At or about two o'clock.
5. Estar loco de alegría	To be overjoyed / over the moon	Estoy loco de alegría	I am overjoyed / I am over the moon.

GRADE 8

ESPAÑOL	INGLÉS	ESPAÑOL	INGLÉS
1. (i) Tener hambre (ii) Tener sed (iii) Tener dolor de	To be hungry To be thirsty To hurt / be sore etc.	Tengo hambre. Tengo sed. Tengo dolor de cabeza.	I am hungry. I am thirsty. I have a headache.
2. Por supuesto	Of course	Soy amable y, por supuesto, inteligente.	I am friendly and, of course, intelligent.
3. A la moda	In the latest fashion	Estoy llevando los pantalones a la moda.	I am wearing pants in the latest fashion.
4. Sin embargo	However	Estoy cansado, sin embargo, voy a estudiar.	I am tired, however, I am going to study.
5. Por el momento	For the time being	Por el momento, sin embargo, tengo que estudiar.	For the time being, however, I have to study.

GRADE 8 cont'd.

ESPAÑOL	INGLÉS	ESPAÑOL	INGLÉS
6. De vez en cuando	From time to time	Me gusta mirar la televisión pero de vez en cuando leo novelas.	I like to watch television but from time to time I read novels.
7. (i) Hoy en día (ii) En la actualidad	Nowadays	Hoy en día tengo muchos quehaceres en casa.	Nowadays I have a lot of chores at home.
8. En efecto	Indeed	Prefiero la bicicleta y en efecto el iPhone.	I prefer the bicycle and indeed the iPhone.
9. Un día sí, otro no	Every other day	Un día sí, otro no, voy al parque.	Every other day, I go to the park.
10. Como de costumbre	As usual	Voy a la escuela por autobús como de costumbre.	I am going to school by bus as usual.

GRADE 9

ESPAÑOL	INGLÉS	ESPAÑOL	INGLÉS
1. A mi entender	In my opinion	A mi entender el fútbol es mejor que el baloncesto.	In my opinion football is better than basketball.
2. Al instante	Instantly	Al instante, llamé a mi madre.	Instantly, I called my mother.
3. Di la mano	I helped	Di la mano al niñito.	I helped the little boy.
4. De sol a sol	From sunrise to sunset	Ayer, yo estudié de sol a sol.	Yesterday, I studied from sunrise to sunset.
5. En un dos por tres	In the blink of an eye	En un dos por tres, él comió la comida.	In the blink of an eye, he ate the food / meal.

GRADE 9 cont'd.

ESPAÑOL	INGLÉS	ESPAÑOL	INGLÉS
6. No pude dar los créditos a los ojos.	I could not believe my eyes	No pude dar los créditos a los ojos cuando vi al joven.	I could not believe my eyes when I saw the young man / youngster.
7. Lo pasé bomba	I enjoyed (myself)	A la fiesta lo pasé bomba a más no poder.	At the party I enjoyed myself to the utmost.
8. Estuve loco de alegría	I was very happy	Estuve loco de alegría cuando recibí el regalo.	I was very happy when I received the present.
9. Sin más ni más	Without delay	Sin más ni más yo fui a mi casa.	Without delay I went to my house.
10. Llorar a lágrima vida	To cry like a baby	Comencé a llorar a lágrima vida.	I began to cry like a baby.
11. (i) De golpe (ii) De repente (iii) De pronto	Suddenly	De golpe, comenzó a llover.	Suddenly, it began to rain.
12. Me quedé de piedra	I was shocked	Me quedé de piedra cuando ella anunció mi nombre.	I was shocked when she announced my name.

www.ingramcontent.com/pod-product-compliance
Ingram Content Group UK Ltd.
Pitfield, Milton Keynes, MK11 3LW, UK
UKHW062000290726
14090UKWH00021B/1311